The **BODY CORPORATE** **HANDBOOK**

The BODY CORPORATE HANDBOOK

A Guide to Buying, Owning and Living in a Strata Scheme or Owners Corporation in Australia

STEPHEN RAFF

Wrightbooks

First published 2009 by Wrightbooks
an imprint of John Wiley & Sons Australia, Ltd
42 McDougall St, Milton Qld 4064

Office also in Melbourne

Typeset in 10.5/13.5pt ITC Giovanni LT

National Library of Australia Cataloguing-in-Publication Data

Author:	Raff, Stephen A.
Title:	The body corporate handbook: a guide to buying, owning and living in a strata scheme or owners corporation in Australia / Stephen Raff
ISBN:	9780731407774 (pbk.)
Notes:	Includes index.
Subjects:	Strata titles — Australia.
	Land titles — Australia.
	Housing management — Australia.
	Real property — Australia.
Dewey number:	346.940433

Printed in Australia by Ligare Book Printer
10 9 8 7 6 5 4 3

Thanks to Lannock Strata Finance & Paul Morton for contributing the material on which table 8.2 is based.

Author photos by Valeriu Campan

Cover images:
Keys on mortgage agreement © Digital Vision
Couple crossing threshold of house © Digital Vision
Senior couple © Digital Vision
Mother hugging young boy © Stockbyte
Scaffolding on apartment building — aqua effect © Photodisc
Builder on site with clients, all in hard hats © Digital Vision
Mixed use development © Matt Davies
High-rise buildings on orange background © Photodisc

Contents

About the author

Stephen Raff is the founder and CEO of Ace Body Corporate Management, an international body corporate management company based in Melbourne. Ace manages over 32 000 units across Australia and Singapore and is responsible for managing property and assets worth over $5 billion. Stephen now supports 70 franchise areas under the Ace name in every state of Australia and the Northern Territory.

Stephen has been on the education subcommittee of Owners Corporation Victoria for the past 12 years, the past five as an office bearer. He is a member of the Institute of Strata Title Management in New South Wales, the Community Titles Institute of South Australia and National Community Titles Institute (NCTI). He has published many articles on body corporate management and legislation in Australia and overseas and is a regular speaker on body corporate and franchising issues here and abroad.

Stephen has lived in and owned strata properties and has been an owner–occupier, an investor and has served on committees of management as a chairperson and a member. He has been in body corporate practice as a manager for over 14 years.

Stephen has a Certificate IV in Assessment and Workplace Training, is a qualified mediator and holds a master's degree in management. He co-authored the bestselling book *Top Franchise CEOs' Secrets Revealed* and has also written the autobiographical book *0–52 Years: Lessons Learnt and Secrets Revealed.*

Stephen lives in Melbourne with his wife and their two children.

For more information about Stephen Raff's consulting services, mediation services, books, CDs or DVDs, or to have him as a guest speaker at your next conference or event, email <stephen.r@acebodycorp.com.au> or visit the Ace website at <www.acebodycorp.com.au>.

Disclaimer

Coverage, terminology, Act and Regulation information pertaining to each state or territory may change from time to time. While every care has been taken, there may be discrepancies and inaccuracies in the information provided here. You should always seek professional advice that is appropriate for your situation. Information contained in this book should be used only as a guide.

Most of the case studies contained in this book represent possible scenarios that could arise and are not based on real people or events. Any relationship to real people or events is purely coincidental. You should seek professional advice specific to your situation (appendix D provides a list of helpful resources).

Acknowledgements

I could not have written this book without the help of many people. Most of them are acknowledged as contributors at the back of the book and I thank them sincerely.

Of course, I would not be in a position to write it without the help of the many people who have assisted me in my career, and especially without the help of the many Ace Body Corporate franchise owners and their employees. Again, my thanks and appreciation to these wonderful people.

I would like to make particular mention of the editor, Matt Davies, for being wonderfully creative and thorough. My special thanks also to Paul Morton, Francesco Andreone, Leslie Clements, Peta Ribbens, Julie McLean, Ian Laird and Tim Graham who provided appreciated advice and feedback along the way.

To my loving wife, Binnie, who has tirelessly supported me throughout my career, is the backbone of my company and the cornerstone of my life.

Preface

In my body corporate management business I meet a lot of people needing help with the many different areas of managing their property. Some are residents in small to medium-sized strata developments; others are managing high-rise apartment blocks with 200 or more units. I have commercial clients who manage retail outlets and others who run office suites, industrial parks and multi-use properties.

While the style of property may differ, the issues tend to be similar: Am I investing in the right kind of property? Will this property suit me? What do I need to know going in? How will I know what's 'my' property and what's considered common property? What sort of fees will I be paying? How can I convince the existing executive committee to make the changes I want? How can I get on the executive committee? What does the executive committee *do* anyway?

I have written this book with mostly residential owner–occupiers and investors in mind, but the majority of the information is just as applicable to tenants and owners of commercial property. I have tried to note where advice or legislation is different for commercial property owners.

How will this book help owners and prospective owners?

Buying a property is an exciting time, but for people buying into a body corporate, there might be some unexpected — and unpleasant — surprises lurking around the corner. Surprisingly, many people don't realise they are buying into a body corporate, often thinking the terms and conditions as well as their lifestyle are exactly the same as if they are buying a 'freehold' property. They don't realise that they will not have the flexibility to make certain alterations to the exterior of their unit, such as painting or installing security doors and outdoor blinds, as all these will have to go through the body corporate for approval. They can't always park their car anywhere they like as there are usually designated parking areas; they may not even be able to maintain the garden in front of their unit because it's considered common property. They may not be allowed to have pets in their property and, if they can, they still may be limited in what type and size of pet they can keep. In a commercial situation, they may have restrictions on how their shop front is constructed or even what colour they can paint the outside.

But there are many benefits, too. Buyers often don't realise that the body corporate's buildings are usually covered under one insurance policy and that there is one common area liability insurance cover as well. So there is no need for individual owners to take out separate building insurance cover for their unit; often the body corporate cover is specific to bodies corporate and normally offers a more expanded cover.

Other areas of common misinformation (or, indeed, no information) are:

- buyer rights when purchasing a property 'off the plan'
- concealed defects that may be hiding within the building structure of their unit

- potential future hidden costs such as galvanised water piping that will eventually need replacing with copper piping

- potentially sharing one water or gas meter that other owners may want to separate (which can be an expensive exercise)

- confusion over fence ownership and suddenly finding you are up for a share of the cost for replacing all the boundary fences on common property

- the absence of money in the administration fund to pay for running the body corporate (including paying for the body corporate insurance!)

- an existing liability claim against the body corporate for a trip, slip or fall claim on common property, for which new owners may have to foot some of the bill (although it would be rare that there would be insufficient liability cover or that the insurance company failed to cover the claim).

These and many other potential issues will be covered in this book, giving existing owners and new buyers a 'heads up' on some of the potential pitfalls that face strata property owners. I have used case studies and other examples throughout to help illustrate points and give you a better insight into how things work.

Having highlighted some of the potential downsides, there are many positive aspects of buying into a body corporate. I have lived in bodies corporate, I've managed them and I've owned units in them. The intention of this book is to provide information. The aim is for you — prospective purchasers and existing unit owners — to use this information to protect yourself and enhance your investment. If you are aware of the traps then you can avoid heartache down the track and ensure that you get value for your purchase dollar.

It's also very important to know what you're in for in terms of lifestyle. Body corporate life is not for everyone; it's a lifestyle choice and may not necessarily suit your personality. Do you like being around other people? Do you want a pet? Does noise affect your sleep? Do you care about reduced flexibility when it comes to property maintenance? Do you mind sharing in costs for running the whole body corporate? Do you mind having restricted parking? These and other questions need to be considered carefully before you decide to buy into the body corporate lifestyle.

Other areas I will cover in this book include:

- pros and cons of investing in strata properties
- state and territory legislation covering bodies corporate
- how to find and buy your ideal property
- how bodies corporate and executive committees operate
- rights and responsibilities associated with owning a strata property (and who pays for them)
- managing disputes
- selling a strata property.

How to use this book

Body corporate laws vary from state to state. Although many of the principles of these laws are common Australia-wide, I have tried to provide comprehensive information for each state so as to give you as much detail as possible about your individual situation.

In each chapter, I have noted where laws deviate from state to state and given examples from a variety of states to help make the information more applicable to a national audience.

Of course, laws change from time to time. Information in this book was up to date at the time of printing, but its currency cannot be guaranteed beyond this time. The best advice I can offer you is to double-check the latest body corporate laws and regulations with your local state-based housing authority (see appendix D for a comprehensive list), your conveyancer, your solicitor or your strata manager.

If you are considering purchasing a strata property, I have no doubt that this book will give you a good understanding of what you must consider before making that purchase. It will provide you with the 'nuts and bolts' of strata living and management. It will help you to understand that different bodies corporate will provide different lifestyles and what you as a purchaser need to consider before diving into body corporate life. As you will come to realise, it takes a particular type of person to live happily in a body corporate, so this book will help you to understand the importance of knowing yourself and recognising whether or not you are suited to this kind of environment.

If you already own or are living in a strata-type property, I hope this book will help you make the most of your life there and equip you with everything you need to know about becoming part of the decision-making committee and what to do if a dispute arises. Because, take it from me, knowledge is power!

Stephen Raff
Melbourne
November 2008

Chapter 1

Is a strata property right for you?

You only have to look around any suburb within 10 to 15 kilometres of an Australian capital city to recognise the increasing popularity of unit-style living. Many buyers love them because it means they can afford a first home or an investment property. Or they can downsize and reduce the burden of maintaining a house with lawn and garden, which means they can have their leisure time, while still enjoying the advantages of inner-city living.

Property developers love to build this style of housing because they can often buy a piece of land with a run-down house on it, demolish the house and build several units on the block, maybe doubling their money in 12 or so months.

But owning a unit, townhouse or apartment is not like owning a house. Because they share common property, they have to be managed by someone. There are also restrictions on what alterations you can make to 'your' home, and you're living in close proximity to your neighbours who may not share the same lifestyle as you.

Australia-wide there are around two million units owned by individuals or companies that are being managed by more than 210 000 bodies corporate (see table 1.1). That's a lot of units affecting a lot of people. It is estimated that more than $1 billion per year is collected and spent by strata and community title schemes around the country.

Why do people live in body corporate properties?

Higher density living has become increasingly popular throughout Australia due to a combination of population growth, housing affordability, security and lifestyle factors. Table 1.1 shows the approximate number of strata properties across the country.

There are more of us than ever before and not everyone wants to live in outlying areas where new estates are being built, so we need to fit more people onto the same area of land. In city areas, that means building skywards. In the suburbs, that means flattening one house and building three or more in its place. For rural or non-capital city dwellers, there tend to be more places available, but prices seem to be going up just as fast as in the city.

All over Australia we are seeing record growth in property values, with Melbourne experiencing a massive 25 per cent increase in house prices in 2007. Brisbane and Adelaide were not far behind, both recording growth of around 20 per cent, according to Australian Property Monitors. The competition has never been fiercer and for first-home buyers, it often means they need to start off with a cheaper strata-type property while they're young and childless and then move on to something bigger once they're financially able, and want a backyard in which to erect a swing set.

Table 1.1: approximate number of strata properties, by region

Region	No. of schemes	No. of units
ACT	4100	33000
NSW	70000	660000
NT	2100	18000
Qld	37000	340000
SA	22000	176000
Tas.	6800	25500
Vic.	65000	500000
WA	55000	275000

Skyrocketing rent prices all over the country have added to this explosive mix, prompting renters to question why they are paying $2000 a month in rent when they could be paying an extra $800 to (eventually) own their own home.

Lifestyle factors are another big driver of this change, with high-rise blocks often providing swimming pools, gyms, saunas, even indoor tennis courts, restaurants, coffee shops and much more. Community-style living is attractive for many single people because it supplies an instant social network with the added bonus of the security of having other people living close by. Young, active people, as well as newly divorced or newly married couples without children, often don't want land because it means time and money spent on maintenance, and they are short of both.

Types of body corporate properties

There are a number of different types of body corporate properties around today. In inner-city areas, medium-rise apartment blocks, such as the one shown in figure 1.1 (overleaf), are becoming more and more popular.

Figure 1.1: medium-rise apartment block

Photo by Matt Davies

Low-rise apartment blocks, such as the one shown in figure 1.2, have been around since the 1960s.

Figure 1.2: a typical low-rise apartment block

Photo by Matt Davies

Also prevalent is the classic 'six-pack' set of units with parking on one side and housing on the other, as shown in figure 1.3.

Figure 1.3: set of six units

Figure 1.4 shows a configuration of attached townhouses, which generally have very little common property.

Figure 1.4: a row of attached townhouses

Double-storey villa units, as shown in figure 1.5 (overleaf), provide space and security for their residents.

Figure 1.5: double-storey villa units

Photo by Matt Davies

Mixed-use developments are springing up more frequently in both cities and outlying suburbs. A typical example is shown in figure 1.6.

Figure 1.6: mixed-use development

Photo by Matt Davies

High-rise apartment blocks, as shown in figure 1.7, are found in most major cities around the world.

Figure 1.7: a high-rise apartment block

Photo by Matt Davies

How have bodies corporate come about?

Up until the 1960s, it was not possible in Australia to hold a title deed for part of a building, storey or air space. That meant it wasn't possible to own a single flat or unit that was part of a group of units. The title-holder owned all buildings and common areas and was not permitted to sell off individual units; they could only be rented out. The only way around this problem was so-called 'company' title where, instead of buying title to a property, you owned a share in a company which gave you the right to use a part of the property. That right was defined under a service agreement.

It wasn't until 'strata title' legislation was introduced first in Victoria (*Transfer of Land (Stratum Estates) Act 1960*), and then in the other states of Australia in the early 1960s, that individuals could hold title to their own apartment or unit and therefore be able to transfer the property without the need for consent. For the first time it became possible, unlike with company title, to hold title for part of land constituting a space between certain levels above or below the surface of land. The word 'strata' came from this legislation (and is the plural of stratum).

Today, strata titles are used to subdivide (by way of a 'strata plan') a building or property into separate 'units' (such as townhouses, multilevel flats or apartments) and used to define common property, such as lawns and gardens, driveways, hallways and lifts. These common property areas are managed by bodies corporate (called 'owners corporations' in some Australian legislation). This governing body is created automatically when the strata plan is registered and all unit owners automatically become members.

Terminology used in this book

Before we go any further, it is probably worthwhile defining some terms used throughout this book. Different states use different terminology, particularly in a legal sense (see table 1.2). The following terms are used throughout this book:

Body corporate—commonly referred to as an owners corporation, community title or strata scheme, a body corporate is the legal entity with responsibility for managing the interests of the members in the common property under its control.

Common property—areas shared by unit owners shown on the plan of subdivision as common property owned by all members in common and managed by the body corporate. Apart from the obvious inclusions like shared driveways, walkways, foyers and lifts, these can also include meeting rooms and various recreational areas such as gyms, swimming pools, tennis courts, even golf courses.

Levies—contributions paid by owners to the body corporate to cover recurring or regular expenditure. These are usually paid quarterly and the amount is generally based on unit entitlement or liability, depending on the state or territory. The term is used interchangeably with 'fees' in this book.

Special levies — one-off fees raised by the body corporate to fund extraordinary major capital expenditure projects, usually as an alternative to having a sinking fund or borrowing.

Strata — the legal term for the subdivisions of property into lots (units) and common property that may apply to multilevel or high-rise buildings, townhouses, factories, offices, storage facilities and even retail units within a body corporate.

Unit entitlement — the proportional share of the body corporate that is owned by each unit holder fixed upon registration of the plan. There are various methods to determine the proportions, but, in general, if your unit is larger, of a higher value or has more amenities, your unit entitlement will also be larger. This gives you both more rights and more responsibilities; you may have a larger proportion of the votes when it comes to a poll vote or, in some cases, a postal ballot for decision making in a general meeting, but you may also be responsible for meeting a larger proportion of the costs.

Units — the apartments/flats/townhouses or other privately owned areas or spaces within a strata subdivision. Often called 'lots' in legislation and also referred to as 'strata properties' in this book.

Table 1.2: common body corporate terminology, by region

Region	'Scheme'	'Body corporate'	'Management committee'	'Manager'
ACT	Unit title or community title	Owners corporation or body corporate	Executive committee or committee of management	Managing agent and unit plan managers

Table 1.2 *(cont'd)*: common body corporate terminology, by region

Region	'Scheme'	'Body corporate'	'Management committee'	'Manager'
NSW	Strata scheme	Owners corporation	Executive committee	Managing agent
NT	Unit title	Management corporation	Committee	Employee or agent
Qld	Community titles scheme	Body corporate	Committee	Body corporate manager
SA	Strata scheme	Strata corporation	Management committee	Agent
Tas.	Strata scheme	Body corporate	Committee of management	Manager
Vic.	Strata plan, plan of subdivision, cluster subdivision plan	Owners corporation	Committee	Manager
WA	Strata scheme	Strata company	Council	Strata manager

Do you want to live in a strata property?

One of the most important decisions you will need to make — before any other — is whether or not buying, living, letting or renting in a body corporate environment is the right choice for you. This may be as an owner–occupier, investor (landlord) or tenant. The reasons for each will vary and are likely to be based on lifestyle, affordability and investment considerations.

If you are going to live in a property (as an owner–occupier or tenant) some of the questions you will want to contemplate are:

- Can I afford to live in this kind of accommodation?

- Will it provide the lifestyle and amenities that I am after (such as social benefits and proximity to other places I want to be)?

- Can I live in a close-knit environment where there may be noise or constant activity?

If you are buying for investment purposes (as an owner–occupier or investor) there are additional questions you will need to ask yourself, including:

- Is the property's value likely to appreciate at a rate I'm happy with?

- What are the maintenance costs on this property likely to be compared with those of another property I'm considering?

- What is the body corporate's financial position? For example, are major expenses likely in the future? How has the corporation decided to fund those expenses? What are the levies?

- Am I looking at a long-term or shorter term investment?

However, before you start to think that the interests of owner–occupiers and investors are so different that they may as well come from different planets, let me highlight the most critical thing that applies to both groups: it's about lifestyle. The lifestyle you expect to enjoy as an owner–occupier is a major component of the purchase price you should be willing to pay. The lifestyle for the person you sell to is a vital factor in the price they will pay (which is the return on your investment). It goes without saying that owner–occupiers are concerned about the value of their investment! For an investor, the lifestyle your tenant expects to enjoy is the critical component of what they will pay you in rent and so of your return on investment. The same is true when you come to sell.

Owner–occupiers should be just as concerned about capital return as they are about lifestyle. And investors should be just as concerned about lifestyle as they are about return on investment. Why? Because they are opposite sides of the same coin. You can't think of one without considering the other.

Living in a body corporate

Life in a body corporate environment is not right for everyone. Some people thrive — attracted to the community-style living (often at a cheaper price than a free-standing house in a similar location) — while others can't stand the close proximity to their neighbours or long for a spacious backyard.

Apartment living in particular is often glorified on television or in movies as being glamorous because characters are depicted as living among a collection of quirky, interesting people. Obviously that's not always the case and some people are in for a rude shock when some of that 'quirkiness' is actually creepiness, rudeness or downright nuttiness.

Others are attracted to the increased security offered by driveway gates (as shown in figure 1.8) or deadlocked exterior doors, or just the fact that there are often more people around in case of danger.

Figure 1.8: security is an important consideration for many strata-property owners

Photo by Matt Davies

Some think unit living will offer a certain lifestyle and sometimes they are disappointed. You may find you don't get along with your new neighbours or never see them because they are either hidden away in their own units or out socialising or working during the hours you're at home.

Living under the same roof as others can be particularly hard to adjust to when you're used to living in a house. As a house owner, you get accustomed to the freedom of doing whatever you want to your property: painting it whatever colour you like; paving wherever you want; establishing garden beds; growing vegetables; heating the pool to a temperature you like; laying a 'floating floor' instead of carpeting. These options are often not open to people owning strata properties. You may find that you need to go through a lengthy approval process to do something that you think should be your own business. You may find you're not even allowed to fire up a barbecue on your balcony or in a courtyard for fear the smell might offend neighbours or the smoke might interfere with someone's clothes drying on a line three metres away. Parking may be too limited for your liking or it might become frustrating that your visitors can't park close to your door. You may come to resent certain decisions about your environment being made by others.

Problems associated with living in close proximity to others might not come from having inconsiderate neighbours, but can arise simply because they are *there*. Just the fact that people are coming and going at all hours, setting alarm clocks, taking showers and starting up their cars may be irritating enough. Their air-conditioners may be noisy, their dodgy plumbing may vibrate through paper-thin walls. Everyone has the right to stay up late, to use the toilet during the night and to undertake shift work—this is all part of community-style living.

But for many people the benefits far outweigh the negatives. I've enjoyed living in an environment where I don't have to think about mowing lawns or make decisions about where to hang my clothes line. The idea of moving into a unit is enticing for many because it might mean they never have to pull out a weed, sweep the driveway or chlorinate the pool. Yes, you have to pay for these benefits (in the form of body corporate fees), but those costs are shared.

Rules, rules, rules

Rules governing the behaviour of residents or tenants are set in two ways: by legislation and by the body corporate creating its own rules of management. Through these rules (also called by-laws) and the dispute resolution process you will be supported if someone is being particularly irritating—you can take action to restore your tranquillity. You may not have the final say in things that affect you, but you certainly have a voice and, if you are an elected member of your body corporate executive committee (voted in at the annual general meeting), that voice will be even louder for the benefit of all members. (Executive committees are discussed further in chapter 7.)

There are other benefits to having rules that guide body-corporate living. In a house, if you object to how your neighbours are behaving or are aggrieved about proposed plans to build a view-blocking monstrosity next door, you are usually on your own. In a body corporate situation, you potentially have an instant team of supporters at your side, ready to do battle against that frustrating neighbour or that property developer.

Law-based rules for living in a body corporate

As mentioned, the rules that apply to those living in strata properties don't originate only from the body corporate and its executive committee; there are also broader federal, state and local laws that apply. There are four levels of body corporate governance in Australia:

- Commonwealth legislation
- state legislation
- local council by-laws
- strata plans legislation, rules and by-laws.

Table 1.3 lists the strata legislation that currently exists in each Australian state and territory.

Table 1.3: strata legislation, by region

Region	Act	Regulations
ACT	*Community Title Act 2001*	Community Title Regulations 2002

15

Table 1.3 *(cont'd)*: **strata legislation, by region**

Region	Act	Regulations
NSW	*Strata Schemes Management Act 1996*	Strata Schemes Management Regulation 2005
	Strata Schemes (Freehold Development) Act 1973	Property, Stock and Business Agents Regulation 2003
	Strata Schemes (Leasehold Developments) Act 1986	
	Property, Stock and Business Agents Act 2002	
	Community Land Management Act 1989	
NT	*Unit Titles Act 2006**	Unit Titles Regulations 2007*
Qld	*Body Corporate and Community Management Act 1997**	Body Corporate and Community Management Regulation 1997*
SA	*Strata Titles Act 1988*	Strata Titles Regulations 2003
	Community Titles Act 1996	Strata Titles (Fees) Regulations 2001
Tas.	*Strata Titles Act 1998*	Strata Titles (Insurance) Regulations 1999
	Fire Service Act 1979	General Fire Regulations 2000
Vic.	*Owners Corporations Act 2006*	Owners Corporations Regulations 2007
	Subdivision Act 1988	Subdivision (Permit and Certification Fees) Regulations 2000
		Subdivision (Procedures) Regulations 2000
		Subdivision (Registrar's Fees) Regulations 2004

Region	Act	Regulations
WA	*Strata Titles Act 1985* *Interpretation Act 1984* *State Administrative* *Tribunal Act 2004*	Strata Titles General Regulations 1996

*These Acts and Regulations were in the process of being amended at the time of printing. The Northern Territory will introduce new legislation (the *Unit Titles Schemes Act*) in 2009.

These Acts and their corresponding Regulations outline specific rules that apply to all manner of strata property features including fences, balconies, air-conditioners, security screens, roofs, walls, floors and ceilings.

Pros and cons

It is difficult to list the positive and negative aspects of unit living as so many of them are subjective. While one person may like the fact they don't have to worry about maintaining the garden outside their front door, others may resent not being able to plant their favourite roses. Table 1.4 sets out common features of living in a strata property; whether they are positive or negative features depends on your point of view! Of course, everything on the list doesn't apply to all types of strata properties.

Table 1.4: pros and cons of living in a strata property

Pros	Cons
High-rise apartments often offer views	Close proximity to neighbours
Increased security	Limited choice on changing the façade and other external features
Minimal exterior maintenance (or at least shared costs)	Increased noise
	Limited parking space

Table 1.4 *(cont'd)*: **pros and cons of living in a strata property**

Pros	Cons
Support of others in disputes	Limited outdoor areas
An instant social network	Possible restrictions on pet ownership
More affordable	
Shared recreational facilities (such as a pool, sauna, spa, gym, jetty, tennis court)	Need to obtain consensus to renovate the building
Reduced maintenance costs	Residents are bound by rules that are deemed to be for the good of all residents.
Restriction on pet ownership	
The opportunity to refurbish to increase the property value at a shared cost	
Residents are bound by rules that are deemed to be for the good of all residents	
New strata commercial and residential properties are green-star rated	
Legislation requires that common property must be maintained at least to the standard it was when the building was registered.	

Cost considerations

Strata properties are often cheaper to buy than a house and indeed cheaper to maintain. But what many buyers need to consider is the cost of body corporate levies (usually paid quarterly) to cover things like maintenance of common property and insurance. What's more, you are reliant on your executive committee to be good asset managers. What if they overlook or fail to anticipate a major cost such as a building defect not covered by insurance, or the legal fees associated with suing the developer over that defect?

Case study: whose responsibility?

John and Eileen were excited about moving into their new inner-city townhouse. Now that their children were fully grown and had moved out of home John and Eileen could finally downsize and afford to move a little closer to town. They'd never owned a brand new place before and were particularly excited about being the first people ever to live in what was a gleaming new two-bedroom unit. John was rapt to be giving away lawn mowing and Eileen was relieved to no longer have to clean a four-bedroom house.

Not long after moving in, John and Eileen discovered that their second-storey balcony had begun to fall away from the house. On closer inspection, they realised that cracking in the mortar had allowed the bolts to become dislodged and, as a result, the whole balcony was literally about to fall down. John immediately contacted the body corporate manager who told him that the moving balcony was not the responsibility of the body corporate because it was not on common property. Also, unfortunately, it was a maintenance issue not claimable under the body corporate's insurance policy. Nevertheless John still insisted that the body corporate manager contact the insurance company. The insurance company was a dead end, saying that because shoddy workmanship was the most likely cause, the issue needed to be addressed with the building developer.

Upon contacting the developer, John was told that this particular company had only taken over the building in the last few months of development, after the initial developer went bust. They claimed to be responsible only for the final internal elements of the buildings such as plastering, painting, fixtures and fittings.

Case study: whose responsibility? *(cont'd)*

Chasing the original developer was just as hopeless. Not only were they bankrupt, they passed the buck back to the final developer who, in turn, passed it back onto the original developer. John felt dizzy from the number of times he had gone round and round in circles.

John sought legal advice. Unfortunately, taking legal action was ruled out after he received advice that, even after spending upwards of $5000 in legal fees, he would most likely be unsuccessful.

In the end, John had the problem fixed himself. And, $3000 later, he was again able to enjoy a twilight drink on his balcony. Although, somehow it didn't taste as good.

Body corporate costs are usually borne by the property owners. Tenants only need to pay the usual bills associated with renting any property, such as electricity, water and gas, if they are separately metered.

Commercial tenants usually pay all outgoings excluding sinking funds (a type of savings fund in which deposits are made regularly to be used later for a specific purpose, such as major unforeseen repairs) and capital items. However, you must always check the leasing agreement.

Test yourself

Sometimes it's difficult to know whether strata property life will suit you. Perhaps you've never lived in close proximity to strangers before or you've never had to deal with much external noise. Below is a series of questions you may want to consider before pulling out your cheque book on auction day.

Self test: suitability for body corporate living

Ask yourself the following questions. If you answer 'yes' to two or more, you may want to reconsider whether body corporate life is for you.

▣ Have you ever lived or stayed in close proximity to other dwellings and not enjoyed it?

▣ Do you mind external noise? Does it bother your sleep?

▣ Are you a 'control freak'? Do you like to have complete control over your surroundings?

▣ Do you need more than one parking bay?

▣ Do you like having a pet?

▣ Are you a private person? Do you like to keep to yourself?

▣ Do you mind living according to someone else's rules?

To get a taste of body corporate life, it might be worthwhile talking to friends or family who live in a unit about the pros and cons. Perhaps you could even stay over for a night or a week to get an idea of what it is like in terms of noise, space and personal freedoms.

Investing in a strata property

We've all heard stories of developers or individuals 'making a killing' on building and selling or buying and selling strata properties, as with other properties. Short-term gains in as little as a couple of years are not unheard of — in 2007 unit values grew by more than 24 per cent in Adelaide, almost 19 per cent in Hobart and almost 15 per cent in Melbourne, according to Australian Property Monitors. Some other property owners can be lucky to see an appreciation of 10 per cent over a number of years, or break even on a purchase price.

CBD living is an increasingly popular proposition in most Australian capital cities, but in some of those cities the cultural shift has been slow to keep pace with the development of high-rise apartments lining our city waterways. Many investors who bought off the plan 10 years ago thinking that city living would be the next big boom in real estate didn't anticipate the slow rate of change. Some didn't realise that it would probably take a good 15 years to make any real money. Others bowed out early at a loss; there were so many apartments available in the early days that once the properties were built, the demand was just not there as quickly as they had anticipated (as the buyers in the following case study discovered).

Case study: choosing the right property

When plans for a series of new high-rise apartments opened up for off-the-plan sales in Melbourne's Docklands precinct, on the water just out of the CBD, Shirley and Roger took notice. It was the late 1990s and all the hype around the area suggested big things to come. Shops, restaurants and bars would open and the area would become Melbourne's new hub. City living with water views, it promised, would go the way of Sydney and investors would be wise to snap up these properties while they were still in the reach of 'mum-and-dad investors'.

Shirley and Roger did just that.

Still about 10 years away from retirement, their plan after buying a two-bedroom unit was to rent it out until they were ready to give up work. By that time, they were convinced, the precinct would be fully up and running and the apartments would be in high demand.

> They would sell their family home and their Docklands investment property, make a killing, and retire to the country.
>
> Six years into the venture (mid 2000s), Shirley and Roger were unimpressed with their investment. They hadn't counted on two things: the abundance of apartments that would be available in the area (empty and available!) and the possibility that the area would take longer to get established than anticipated (or promised by the developers, at least).

Choosing the right property for purchase is discussed further in chapter 2.

Becoming a landlord

The other aspect of investing in a unit that you will need to consider is the fact that you will become a landlord. If you haven't had this responsibility before, there are a couple of things to do with managing a rental property that you should consider.

Many investors choose to ask a real estate agent or another private agent to manage the property for them. This will usually cost around 7 to 9 per cent of your rental income (plus GST) in exchange for processing your rental payments, processing tenant applications, setting up the lease agreement, organising tradespeople to make repairs to the property as needed, and dealing with tenant issues once the property is leased.

If you choose to manage the property yourself, you will have to take care of all these aspects on your own. And, whether you go through an agent or not, you will still have to pay for marketing the property (to find tenants), landlord's insurance (to cover the building, fixtures and fittings), annual land tax, council rates and ongoing services, such as water and sewerage service charges (real estate agents can pay these for you out of the rent, on request).

The lessee's bond is held by a third party such as a state-based Residential Tenancies Bond Authority. For further information contact your state's real estate authority (see appendix D for a contact list).

What next?

Now that you're sure buying into a strata property is for you, chapter 2 outlines what you need to consider when searching for your ideal unit.

Chapter 2

Seeking out that perfect place

Now that you've decided you want to buy and/or live in a strata property, it's time to begin the hunt. Searching for real estate can be an emotional journey; the excitement and nervousness of bidding at auctions, the disappointment of missing out on places you have already fallen in love with. Finding nothing you like, finding too many places you like. Finding that cute little place that has so much going for it (if only it was a little closer to the train station or had a private courtyard).

For commercial property, you will need a space that suits your planned business use. This will probably include the right amount of floor space, customer/client parking, kitchenette and toilet facilities, and, of course, location. A high-exposure spot might be important for your business.

Making a list of what you want before you set out is always a good idea. For residential property, think about location (including proximity to amenities you will want to access), number of bedrooms, size of block (such as ground-level free-standing units, a semi-detached townhouse or high-rise apartment block), and other things that might be particularly important to you such as a courtyard, pool or lock-up garage.

These days, the internet takes a lot of the travel time out of a property search. When I bought my first home, it was a case of getting up early on a Saturday morning, trawling through the paper for houses to buy and spending the whole weekend cruising around the 'burbs looking at places. These days you can input property features into websites such as <www.domain.com.au> and <www.realestate.com.au> and view photos of the properties in your price range from your work or home computer. When I started, we were lucky if the newspaper ad carried a sketch of the façade!

Make a checklist

As anyone who's ever bought property knows, it's hard to find everything you want in one place (particularly for the price you're willing to spend!). Build some flexibility into your list of features. Start with the 'must haves' and work your way down to the 'like to haves'. Your 'must haves' might include two bedrooms, undercover parking and some private outdoor space. Your 'like to haves' might be a gym, carport or second bathroom.

Be firm with your 'must haves'. If the property looks beautiful in the ad and seems within your price range but isn't walking distance from public transport, for example, don't even bother considering it. You will only end up wasting your own time. But be flexible on other features. So it's at the front of the block and not the back? Maybe the street is not very busy and traffic noise will be minimal, or it has a high fence or big trees that will give you added privacy.

And, of course, write down the maximum you can afford to pay and stick to it (but make sure the property is worth it as well!).

A sample checklist is provided in table 2.1.

Table 2.1: example property search checklist

Property address:	
Must haves	**✓ or ✗**
Close proximity to public transport (within 1 km)	
Close proximity to shops (within 1 km)	
Courtyard/balcony	
2 bedrooms	
Off-street parking	
Pets allowed	
Separate facilities (water, gas and power)	
Score:	
Like to haves	**✓ or ✗**
3 bedrooms	
Second bathroom	
High fence	
Lock-up garage	
Visitor parking	
Quiet street	
Walking distance to beach (within 1 km)	
Large trees	
Cable TV	
Score:	

Research, research, research

The importance of research cannot be stressed enough. Once you know the type of properties you want, you need to do your homework. Start looking at price patterns of the past few years in areas you like and make notes on how big properties were, where they were located and what they sold for. You can check auction sale prices in major Sunday papers; otherwise real estate agents are usually happy to disclose prices when they know you're serious about buying. Publicly available databases such as Australian Property Monitors <www.apm.com.au> and Residex <www.residex.com.au> are also worth a look.

Take your time in looking. Assuming you're not in a rush because you've already sold your current home or are about to be evicted, spend as many Saturdays as you can looking inside places, going to auctions and watching results in the paper. These days there are usually inspection times during the week as well. The search process is all learning and will better equip you to make the best decision when your ideal property comes up.

Be organised, too. Depending on how particular you are about the way you manage your life, it might be helpful to make a spreadsheet of places you've looked at. Give them a mark out of 10, note what's good and bad about them and record their ultimate selling price (it's also a good idea to compare the quoted price to the actual selling price). But remember, this is a research tool, not something to look back on and use as an excuse to berate yourself over a property you chose not to bid on or missed out on by a couple of thousand dollars. You will fast become an expert on what you can expect to get for your money.

Know your target area intimately. When you look up an address, it will save you a lot of time if you know what's nearby. How close are the shops, schools and bus stops?

And another thing you probably already know, but it's worth mentioning anyway: don't believe everything the real estate agent tells you. Although they may appear nice, friendly and even helpful, always remember that they work for the seller, not for you the buyer. It's their job to sell the unit for the vendor, not to reveal potential negatives to buyers. While you may have some recourse against developers for inferior workmanship, you are on your own when it comes to what real estate agents tell you. Unless it's in the legal documents pertaining to the sale, be wary of what they promise.

Table 2.2 lists the documents that vendors must provide in each state and territory alongside the contract of sale and certificate of title.

Table 2.2: vendor disclosure documents, by region

Region	Vendor disclosure documents
ACT	Building reports, pest compliance, energy rating
NT	Not mandatory
	Section 37 search (generally prepared by the manager)
NSW	Section 109 certificate (disclosure of current executive committee, insurance, managing agent, levies and when they are due. Generally prepared by the manager)
	Contract of sale
Qld	Section 206 Body Corporate Disclosure statement (information about insurance and balance of the sinking fund, any engineers' reports or any defects — generally completed by the manager at the request of the purchaser)
	Section 205 of the *Body Corporate and Community Management Act 1997* requires a body corporate to issue a Body Corporate Information Certificate and to make its records available
SA	Vendor's statement (Section 7)
	Section 41 of the Strata Titles Act (prepared by the manager)
	Section 139 of the Community Titles Act (generally prepared by the manager)

Table 2.2 *(cont'd)*: **vendor disclosure documents, by region**

Region	Vendor disclosure documents
Tas.	Vendor statement
	Strata title statement
	Section 83 (5) (generally prepared by the manager or the solicitor)
Vic.	Owners Corporation Certificate (generally prepared by the manager)
	Vendor's statement (Section 32)
WA	Section 43 certificate (generally prepared by the manager)
	Forms 28 & 29 (generally prepared by the vendor or the vendor's agent)

An agent might say, for example, that car lot 10 belongs to unit one, when in actual fact it doesn't and in some cases there will be no car lot attached to the unit at all. Another example might be that the agent tells you that the backyard belongs to your title and you accept this because it is all fenced in, when in actual fact, despite the fence, it is common property and belongs to the body corporate.

Strata inspections

In some states, including New South Wales and Queensland, professional strata inspections or 'strata reports' can be arranged through companies such as Purchasers Strata Inspections Pty Ltd (see <www.strata.com.au>). For a fee, these companies can search the records of the body corporate and other information related to a body corporate you are thinking of buying into. They can tell you if the body corporate holds adequate insurance cover and whether they comply with fire regulations, for example.

Strata management plans

Many new developments are combining residential and commercial units by locating private living spaces on top of a strip of shops, restaurants or other businesses. In this case, there should be a strata management plan, building management committee or appropriate by-laws in place. This document sets out the way a building will operate when sharing with areas that are not part of the same strata scheme. It defines how the whole complex will work together including governance and cost sharing. This may also apply to areas that contain a number of apartment blocks, all on different schemes.

Not enough buyers are aware of this document (although it's not available in all states and territories) which becomes very important when you consider it may be the one thing that determines how well your block is going to function into the future. Where available, they may come under different names, such as:

- community management statement (Queensland)
- strata management statement (New South Wales)
- management statement (Tasmania)
- forms numbered OC1 and OC2 (Victoria).

A strata management plan may set out:

- the responsibilities of the body corporate
- the division of power between strata occupying the same site
- how common property may be used
- asset ownership between strata
- any contractual agreements with outside parties

↳ individual owner entitlements that determine levies and
voting rights.

Local planning issues

Driving around your target suburbs, you will get an idea of
what the local council considers to be good planning. If you
are presented with a mismatch of older style houses, modern
square boxes, low-rise apartments, townhouses and small
commercial sites, you can pretty much assume the council has
declared a virtual free-for-all when it comes to planning and
could approve even the most inappropriate of structures right
next to where you want to buy. It is worth checking out any
zoning or other restrictions in your target area as well and any
plans for new roads, car parks, shopping areas and the like.
That beautiful city, park or water view may become a prefab
concrete wall within 12 months of you moving in and there
might be nothing you can do about it.

Case study: investigating the land around you

Gayle and Ian were the excited new owners of a gorgeous hillside
apartment with sweeping views of the ocean. It had always been
their dream to buy near the water and, when Ian was offered an
attractive early-retirement package, they jumped at the chance
to retire by the sea. They managed to pick up a second-storey
apartment with just enough height to give them a clear view of the
water over some fully grown pine trees and a caravan park that sat
on the water's edge.

Two years into their retirement, things had been going well.
They had settled nicely into their new community, made plenty
of friends and felt their health had never been better. Then
disaster struck. The caravan park owner sold his land to a

---

developer who submitted plans to build a six-storey building with shops on the ground floor and private accommodation in the top five stories. Although located further down the hill, the height of the planned development would fully obstruct Gayle and Ian's ocean view forever. Not only would their property value plummet, their gorgeous view—the reason they bought the apartment in the first place—would be gone.

Gayle and Ian pleaded with the council to reconsider their decision to issue a planning permit to the developers. The council declined, saying that the development would be great for the town and attract more tourists to the area. The council stated that the development would make the town more vibrant, economically sound and, in fact, increase the value of everyone's properties.

Gayle and Ian didn't agree, but their hands were tied. They put their property on the market and hoped for the best.

You may also want to check with the council to see if there are:

- heritage overlays
- height controls
- 100-year flood overlays (meaning the property is likely to experience a flood once every 100 years because of its location)
- a water management plan (see box overleaf)
- renewable energy requirements (see box on p. 35).

Any of these planning conditions may have an impact on what you can and can't do, not only to your building but also to the surrounding properties.

Water management plans

This box explains water management plans and how they relate to new and existing bodies corporate.

New body corporate

The sustainable water plan will come packaged as part of a planning requirement. Developers in most states and territories must implement one or more sustainable measures. In New South Wales (and in 90 per cent of cases elsewhere) they install water tanks for both common and private property.

Members of a new development generally inherit a system that is in place for landscape watering and recycled water for cisterns. The body corporate will require a low-level environmental health plan for this system that will ensure routine checking of the collection and filtration devices. When the tanks are empty the body corporate will purchase water from the local water authority (this may also be at a premium).

A larger complex may have grey water as well as rain water collection and a treatment plant for gardens, washing cars, laundry use, but not for kitchen and shower use (for further information on allowable uses consult your local EPA). You would need a documented environmental health plan for this system that will ensure routine testing and treatment of the collected water. There may be reporting of water quality results by your local EPA or council.

An eco-village type complex will also include a black water treatment plant. So far these are only installed with special permission and have strict environmental reporting and monitoring requirements. It will be some time before a decentralised black water treatment plant is commonplace in a body corporate.

Existing body corporate

Existing bodies corporate have the same management requirements but have to install the systems themselves and will need to calculate the costs involved. The good news is that the energy savings involved usually have an impact on the economics of the project. If the body corporate borrows to retro-fit the building, often the savings come close to meeting the loan repayments.

The body corporate will need to undertake an audit of consumption, wastage and need in order to determine the required size of the tanks and equipment. For instance, the complex may contain a pool and in order to provide the 'top up' requirements tanks might have to be installed rather than trucking in water. The body corporate will also need to install back-flow valves for safety reasons.

Renewable energy

This box explains renewable energy plans and how they relate to new and exisiting bodies corporate.

New body corporate

Renewable energy options will be installed as part of a planning requirement or marketing attraction. So far, these include solar power and gas-boosted hot water, wind turbines and cogeneration. The option may include retaining all the power for the site and/or selling back to the national or state grid.

In order to provide a service like this the body corporate will have an embedded network and may become an exempt power retailer. By becoming a retailer the body corporate can purchase and resell power to only their consumers (body corporate). Legislation in most states prevents the body corporate selling the power to the consumer at price per kWh greater than market price. The benefit to owners will be reduced cost per kWh of electricity.

Existing body corporate

Retro-fitting of existing buildings and/or sites will be based on financial considerations, pay-back periods and return on investment.

Renewable energy (cont'd)

It is more likely to be the driver in large (over 100 units) buildings or complexes. Smaller complexes are more likely to look at stand-alone solutions such as solar hot water and solar lights or purchasing 'green' power from their power retailer.

Currently Australian governments do not recognise 'strata' as an approved entity to apply for assistance in conversion. If and when governments offer such rebates it will assist in sharing the cost of supplying the infrastructure, reducing the carbon footprint of the building and benefiting all the community. However, there's no need to wait for governments—investigate the financial economics yourself and you'll probably find that the energy savings go a substantial way to meeting the repayments on funding the retro-fit.

Buying off the plan

Buying off the plan means buying a property before it's constructed (see figure 2.1 on p. 38). Purchasing this way can save on stamp duty and other costs. If you're looking to buy a property off the plan—that is, to buy your unit or apartment based on viewing the printed designs or a showroom mock-up before the place is actually constructed or completed—consider the following:

- Is what you're looking at the final, approved plans?

- Don't look just at the layout of your preferred unit; also look at your neighbours' layout. Will your bedroom abut their lounge room or bathroom? Could this add to noise levels in rooms where you really don't want it?

- You will need to identify if it is a single, multiple or layered scheme and, if it is a staged scheme built over so many years, how all this will affect your purchase.

- Investigate the developer, asking to see other properties they've constructed. You could even contact consumer affairs or the Office of Fair Trading in the state or territory in which you're buying to make sure there have been no complaints made about that particular company or individual.

- There are tax benefits associated with buying off the plan; ask your accountant where you can claim reductions.

- Is there an opportunity to get the fit-out and colour scheme that you want?

- Be wary of schemes that guarantee a rental return, as sometimes the guarantee is only for a limited period and you may have a mortgage to maintain over 20 to 30 years. Also, you may be effectively paying for the rental guarantee by paying a higher market value price for the unit.

- Check with the local real estate agent to see what rental returns similar properties are achieving.

- Who is the developer? Do they have a good reputation? What about the builder?

- Developers can vary the plan by up to 10 per cent without consent.

- Prospective purchasers don't have to pay a 10 per cent deposit — you can obtain a bank deposit bond which is like a bank guarantee for the deposit and pay interest on the deposit amount.

- READ THE CONTRACT!

Figure 2.1: buying off the plan before construction is complete

Photo by Matt Davies

Checking out the title

Although names vary, there are basically two types of title for strata properties: strata title and company title.

Strata title

Strata title is the more common and straightforward title that can be applied to flats, units, apartments, office buildings, factories and the like. This title gives you ownership of a part of a larger property based on the horizontal and vertical subdivision of 'air space'. Owners have a certificate of title, are absolute owners of a freehold unit and have an undivided share of the common property. You are free to occupy, lease (rent) or sell the property at your own discretion and you are automatically a member of the body corporate with this type of real property.

Be aware that in some cases the body corporate may have obligations contained within the planning permit such as clauses that prevent people aged under 55 years or people with children living with them from buying into the body corporate. There can also be a clause not allowing short-term rental, such as less than three months, or one stipulating that the unit may not be used as a principal place of residence.

Company title

Company title is a property title that applies when the owner or owners of a property that consists of two or more self-contained dwellings form a company. This is usually done prior to the property being constructed. A group of shares in the company is issued for each unit and the constitution of the company provides that a holding of a group of shares comes with the entitlement to occupy one of the units. The shareholders are therefore the members of the private company that owns the property and which is governed by company law as opposed to strata legislation (making the legislation uniform across Australia).

The negatives of buying into a company title need to be carefully balanced against the positives. They can be more difficult to sell and it can be hard to find finance. Also, there may be restrictions in the company's constitution on renting them. What often makes them so tricky to sell is the fact that the board of directors may be entitled under the constitution to approve any potential buyer. In effect, if the board don't like you, they can prohibit the vendor from selling their shares. But, in practice, this rarely happens. However, specialist legal advice is usually required.

For investors, renting out a company-title unit can be difficult (if they let you at all!) because potential tenants may have to go through the same process of scrutiny as buyers. In some cases, you may be able to rent it out only to a pre-approved list of people (which may include family members, for example).

In the past, loans have tended to be more difficult to secure on properties with a company title because the lending institution doesn't get the mortgage security of a land title. Instead, they get a charge over shares with exclusive use of a lot attached to them (subject to the approval of the board of directors). To cover these obstacles, banks have often only let buyers borrow up to 60 per cent of the property value. This is slowly changing and has improved over the past 20 years.

These difficulties, however, sometimes mean company-title properties can be a little cheaper than equivalent units being sold under a strata title so might appear more attractive to an owner–occupier. You may have noticed there are some really wonderful old buildings in interesting areas that make up in lifestyle any disadvantages of title.

Company title is rare these days and you can covert to a strata title if you have unanimous agreement from members. The application process can be complex and there will be stamp duty and capital gains tax implications. You will therefore need to seek specialist legal advice. This can be costly but conversion can significantly enhance the value of units in the scheme.

There are more than these two types of title that cover strata properties in Australia. These include:

- Australian Capital Territory — unit plan, community association plan, company title
- New South Wales — strata plan, neighbourhood plan, community title plan, company title, stratum title
- Northern Territory — unit plan, company title
- Queensland — building format plans, standard format plan, volumetric plan, company title
- South Australia — strata plan, primary strata plan, community title plan, company title

- Tasmania — strata plan, community schemes, stage development schemes, company title

- Victoria — cluster plans, strata plans, plan of subdivision, company share, stratum title

- Western Australia — strata plan, survey strata plan, company title.

Investigating body corporate records

Before you commit your hard-earned cash to a particular unit, it's worth checking the body corporate records in that unit's state or territory. These records can sometimes reveal disturbing details about the state of the building, its management and its finances. The main things you should look out for are:

- whether the body corporate is active

- how may bodies corporate affect the property

- the body corporate's budget, to see the financial status of the body corporate and if any significant special levies have been struck

- whether there is any litigation afoot or contemplated

- whether any defects have been identified in the building

- whether current and appropriate levels of insurances are in place

- the amount of levies that each unit owner pays, and whether any members are in arrears

- the ratio of residential owners to tenants (for example, 17 renters in a block of 18 units might create a high cost of wear and tear to the common property areas due to the transient nature of tenants constantly moving in and out)

- the body corporate's view on pets
- the rules of the body corporate, to see if they are valid and up to date, and to give an indication of how the body corporate operates.

The law varies from state to state about the extent to which purchasers can access information. Table 2.3 summarises what's available around the country while appendix C gives a more detailed explanation for each state and territory.

Table 2.3: searches and disclosures, by region

Region	Can scheme records be inspected?	General access requirements	Where are strata or other plans recorded?	Does this information need to be provided for sales?
ACT	Yes	Owner's consent	ACT Planning and Land Authority	Yes
NT	Yes	Owner's consent	Land Titles Office and Building Board	Yes
NSW	Yes	Owner's consent	Department of Lands	Yes
Qld	Yes	Owner's consent	Department of Natural Resources & Mines	Yes
SA	Yes	Owner's consent	Land Titles Office	Yes
Tas.	No	Nothing in the Act	Land Titles Office	No

Region	Can scheme records be inspected?	General access requirements	Where are strata or other plans recorded?	Does this information need to be provided for sales?
Vic.	Yes	With owner's or mortgagee's consent	Land Victoria	Yes
WA	Yes	With owner's or mortgagee's consent	Land Gate	Yes

Source: Adapted from NCTI. Additional tables and information are available from the National Community Titles Institute website. Visit <www.ncti.org.au>.

Insurance

One area that is particularly important to investigate properly is the body corporate's insurance cover. You want to find out which company holds the policy, the valuation amount and when it was last valued. You don't want to find yourself in a situation where the whole block burns down and, because its last valuation was years ago, you're not entitled to the current cost of restoring your unit to its original condition. In most states and territories (except for Western Australia and Tasmania) you are legally entitled to this information.

Narrowing down your investment options

If you're looking around purely for an investment, there are a number of things to consider. From a financial standpoint, you will need to ask yourself:

- Will the lifestyle the property provides be attractive to a renter and to a potential purchaser when you come to sell?

- Will the rent cover the mortgage payments (or as closely as you want them to)?

- What will be the term of the mortgage?

- How will the mortgage be financed?

- Will there be any tax benefits associated with negative gearing?

- Will the tax benefits be worth your while?

- How should you buy the property? Under your own name, jointly with a partner, or through a trust account or a super fund?

Consulting a financial planner is the best way to answer these questions for your specific circumstances. Visit the Financial Planning Association website at <www.fpa.asn.au> to locate a planner in your area.

As when investing in any property — house, factory or unit — location is important. How easy will it be to find a tenant? What kind of tenant will you attract in that particular area? And it's not only the suburb that's important, but the specific location within that suburb as well — right down to the street and, in some cases, which side of the street.

Property-buying checklist for investors and live-in investors

This box outlines things to consider when property shopping for investors or live-in investors.

Location

Suburb desirability is extremely important. Will people want to rent there? Are property values in the area on the rise?

What else is happening in that street? What is the condition of other properties around it? Are people in the street 'house proud' or would you be surrounded by long grass and beaten-up cars in the front yard? Is the property you're interested in surrounded by old houses that are likely to be bought, bulldozed and replaced with undesirable blocks that could threaten the value of yours?

Is the unit close to work, recreational facilities, supermarkets, shopping centres, schools, beaches, city and public transport?

Quality

Standard of construction: Does the structure seem sound or are there cracks in the walls, uneven floors or rising damp in the walls?

Quality of fixtures and fittings: Has the unit been fitted out well or does it seem to be finished off with cheap materials? This may deter renters, or buyers when it comes to resale.

Body corporate finances

What are the council rates, annual fees and special levies? Have you budgeted for these? What if they increase?

Does the body corporate owe any money? Ask to see its financial statements.

Is there a sinking or maintenance fund?

Plan of subdivision

Are the property measurements the same as what's stated in the plan of subdivision and contract of sale? (Check both unit and car spaces.)

Is the car parking space part of the title or common property? If it is a 'lot' on your title, ensure it is transferred with the title. If it's considered common property, is there a lease or licence in place?

Property-buying checklist for investors and live-in investors (cont'd)

Management

Who manages the property? Does the manager/caretaker live on site?

What is the grievance procedure? Have any complaints been logged at the body corporate meetings? Ask to see a copy of the minutes of previous meetings.

What are the 'rules' in this body corporate?

Is there any pending legal action against the body corporate?

Has there been any resolved legal action against the body corporate or the building itself? Any tribunal decisions will be registered with the Australasian Legal Information Institute. Check its website at <www.austlii.edu.au>.

Maintenance

Is there a maintenance plan for the site? Ask to see a copy.

Are there any current or planned building works or large-scale maintenance? Is this cost already covered or will a special levy be imposed in the future?

Are there any obvious structural defects? If you are concerned, you may want to consider getting a report from a building surveyor or architect before signing.

As when making any investment, it is important to keep your thinking as financially focused as you can. It's not whether you would enjoy living there, it's whether someone else will want to live there and pay you rent. Does it really matter if you don't like the colour of the kitchen or the style of the tiles?

Not at all! But it does matter whether someone else will want to rent it or buy it at a future date.

What can I afford to spend?

Finding your perfect place is one thing, being able to afford it is another. There are four things to consider here:

- how much you can borrow
- if you're eligible for any government grants
- how much you have for your initial deposit
- if you can afford the ongoing fees associated with the property.

How much can I borrow?

It's a sad reality that, during 2008, around one in five Australian homeowners were under 'mortgage stress', meaning they were falling into arrears, considering selling or facing default proceedings. This equated to around 750 000 Australian households, with about 300 000 under 'severe' stress, according to Fujitsu Consulting 2008, *The Anatomy of Australian Mortgage Stress*. Defaults and voluntary sales were highest in New South Wales, followed by Victoria. Western Australia had the highest proportion of households refinancing.

In my view, there are two reasons for this: interest rate increases and people borrowing beyond their means. It used to be that you had to have a 20 per cent deposit to apply for a home loan; these days in some cases you can borrow 100 per cent of the property value or even more (to cover taxes and other purchasing costs). All you have to do is take out mortgage insurance (which costs more money). The trouble is that the insurance covers the lender, not the borrower. If you can't make your ongoing repayments, you're forced to sell.

The answer to this is drawing up a budget. There is plenty of help out there to assist you in determining how much you can comfortably borrow. Websites such as Mortgage Choice <www.mortgagechoice.com.au> help you calculate how much you can afford to borrow based on your current savings and costs, what you could afford to repay each month, interest rates, the period of the loan and which state you live in. If you prefer a more personal service, visit your accountant or ask a friend to recommend one.

Home loans

Borrowing money to buy a property is a daunting prospect for a lot of people, especially the first time they have to do it. The concept of going into debt just doesn't sit well with many of us. But let's be real, for most of us, if we want to own our own home, borrowing is the only way to achieve it.

However much we might like to think that debt is bad, the fact is that debt is an enabler. With debt, we can achieve our dreams. The trick is not to avoid debt, but to ensure that you manage it and not allow it to take control of you.

But how do you go about it? There seem to be so many options these days: banks, other lending institutions, mortgage brokers. There are more than 1000 different home loans available in Australia — where do you start? Again, research is the key. The more you know, the more informed your ultimate decision will be. Home loans are never simple and, although the basic interest rate may seem low when you compare one with another, you still need to take account of establishment fees, loan-breaking fees and ongoing 'administration' fees. Don't just naively think that the advertised rate is what you'll pay. To compare apples with apples, you need to turn all these fees into an 'interest rate equivalent'. The 'consumer comparison rate' promoted by consumer advocates is a good start, but remember, even this calculation under quotes the rates as it excludes all government fees and charges!

Thankfully, there are websites such as Mortgage Choice <www.mortagechoice.com.au> and brokers such as eChoice <www.echoice.com.au>, Aussie <www.aussie.com.au> and Wizard Home Loans <www.wizard.com.au> who do the work for you. They have software programs that compare the rates in their entirety, considering all the extra costs and benefits associated with the loans. Does the loan have a redraw facility, or offer a fee-free savings account with it or a reduced-rate credit card? Do they insist you open a savings account with the lender (which has fees attached to it) in order to access a loan?

So why not let a broker do the shopping around for you? It doesn't cost you any extra, they visit your home, offer a variety of loan options and oversee the paperwork process.

Government help for first home buyers

The First Home Owner Grant (FHOG) scheme was introduced on 1 July 2000, originally to offset the effect of the GST on home ownership. It is a national scheme funded through each state and territory and administered under their own legislation.

Under the scheme, a one-off grant of up to $14 000 (for established homes) or $21 000 (for new homes) is payable to first home buyers who satisfy all the eligibility criteria. (Note that these grants are slated to decrease back down to $7000 and $14 000 respectively after June 2009.)

The broad principles of the grant are:

- At least one of the applicants must be an Australian citizen or have permanent residency in Australia.

- Applicants must be aged over 18 and buying or building their first home in Australia.

- To qualify for assistance, neither the applicant nor their partner can have owned a home in Australia prior to

1 July 2000, either jointly, separately or with some other person, or purchased a home on or after 1 July 2000 and occupied that home.

⊷ The home must be located in Australia.

⊷ The home must be intended to be a principal place of residence and occupied for a continuous period of six months commencing within 12 months of completion of the transaction (settlement or completion of construction).

⊷ Joint applicants are restricted to a single application for a single property and only one grant is made.

⊷ The grant is not means tested.

Table 2.4 sets out how to access the FHOG in your state or territory. (Note: a list of 'approved agents' is contained on each website.)

Table 2.4: accessing the First Home Owner Grant, by region

Region	Administering body	Website	Where do I obtain and lodge my application?
ACT	ACT Revenue Office	<www.revenue.act.gov.au>	Approved agent or ACT Revenue Office
NSW	Office of State Revenue	<www.osr.nsw.gov.au>	Approved agent or the Office of State Revenue
NT	Territory Revenue Office	<www.revenue.nt.gov.au>	Approved agent (most lending institutions) or Territory Revenue Office

Region	Administering body	Website	Where do I obtain and lodge my application?
Qld	Office of State Revenue	<www.osr.qld. gov.au>	Approved agent or the Office of State Revenue
SA	Revenue SA	<www.revenuesa. sa.gov.au>	Approved agent or Revenue SA
Tas.	State Revenue Office	<www.treasury. tas.gov.au>	Approved agent or any Service Tasmania shop
Vic.	State Revenue Office	<www.sro.vic. gov.au>	Approved agent or the State Revenue Office
WA	Office of State Revenue	<www.dtf. wa.gov.au>	Approved agent or the Office of State Revenue

Payments are made via electronic funds transfer (EFT) at settlement (when buying an existing home), on the first drawdown of the loan (in the case of a contract to build) or after sighting of the Certificate of Occupancy (for owner–builders).

For more information on the national First Home Owners Grant visit <www.firsthome.gov.au>.

Some states, namely New South Wales, Queensland and Victoria, offer additional concessions to first home buyers as outlined below.

New South Wales

The New South Wales First Home Plus Scheme provides exemptions or concessions on transfer duty and mortgage

51

duty for eligible first home buyers on top of the FHOG. This includes vacant land on which you intend to build your first home.

There are no income or assets tests to qualify for the benefits. It provides eligible purchasers with exemptions on transfer duty and mortgage duty on homes valued up to $500 000 and concessions on duty for homes valued between $500 000 and $600 000. There are no additional 'duties' (taxes) applied, irrespective of the amount of the advance. Visit <www.osr.nsw.gov.au> for more information about this scheme.

Queensland

In Queensland, people who buy their first home may also be eligible for a transfer duty and mortgage duty concession.

In addition to the first home concession, home concessions exist for the purchase of a home that is not a first home. From 1 January 2009 mortgage duty will be abolished in full. See <www.osr.qld.gov.au> for more information.

Victoria

In Victoria, the First Home Bonus, in addition to the federal FHOG, is available to eligible applicants buying their first home. The scheme offers a bonus of $3000 for existing homes or $5000 for new homes valued up to $500 000.

In addition, the Regional First Home Bonus provides an additional $3000 to first home buyers purchasing newly constructed homes in regional Victoria until 30 June 2009. The regional bonus is on top of the $14 000 FHOG and the $5000 bonus for newly constructed homes. This means an eligible first home buyer in regional Victoria is entitled to receive a total of $29 000 in cash-grant assistance towards their first home. See <www.sro.vic.gov.au> for eligibility details.

How much should you spend?

Recent surges in property prices, particularly in capital cities, have lured investors to jump into investing in a strata property with the prospect of quick profits. But this is not as easy as your local newspaper or reality TV show makes it sound.

For owner–occupiers, I would always advise buying within your price range. It sounds obvious, but this means weighing up how much money you need to live on and what your repayments will be (allowing for a few interest rate rises), not just what the lenders say you can borrow (see previous section, 'How much can I borrow?'). They are not necessarily as concerned as you should be about how much they will lend to you. They'll always get their money back one way or another, but you may not always have a place to go home to.

Spending too little on a small, one-bedroom place in an outer-city location that might seem like a bargain at the time may end up not saving you any money at all. You may have to travel further to get to the places you want to go, which can be extremely costly with increasing petrol prices, and you are more likely to end up unhappy with your purchase. If you change your mind, a quick sale on an outlying unit is likely to *cost* you money rather than making any.

Spending too much has its obvious downsides too. Scrimping for every last penny in order to make your mortgage payments will limit what you can afford to do in your leisure time. And, although you live close to great shops and cafés, what's the point if you can't afford to buy new clothes or eat out? Lifestyle is a big consideration and a major component of 'what you can afford'.

Market forces are difficult to predict. Will interest rates go up? Will property prices increase or plateau for a while? Not even the so-called experts ever seem to be able to agree. Therefore, the best advice is to not budget too tightly and give yourself some breathing space.

For more information about budgeting, see <www.money manager.com.au> or <www.community.gov.au> under 'Community Information & Services' > 'Financial'.

What next?

Now that you know where you want to buy, how much you have to spend and what the market is doing in your target area, it's time to carry out due diligence by researching and investigating the physical state of the unit in your chosen strata block. Chapter 3 outlines what else you'll need to know now that you've found that perfect unit.

Assessing the building and surrounding property

So you've looked and looked and finally found a place you're really excited about. You can easily picture yourself living there. It seems to be within your price range, has everything on your 'must have' list and a few features on your 'like to have' list.

You thought finding it was hard? There's still plenty to do.

What to look for

Properties generally look their best when real estate agents are involved. Flaws are minimised and features are highlighted. Sellers even resort to hiring different furniture or creating homely smells such as freshly baked bread to craft a certain atmosphere that might appeal to their target buyer. Cut flowers displayed in vases are common.

If you're particularly serious about a property, go and check it out at different times of the day. Does the street get busy during peak hour? Do delivery trucks use that street on their way to nearby shops? Are there people hanging around in the street after dark? You could even visit the local police station and ask if they have any trouble in that particular area.

See if you can find out where rooms in your place are situated in relation to your neighbours. As when buying off the plan, you want to make sure where you sleep doesn't line up with next door's television or toilet.

Once inside, do a thorough check. Try not to be too dazzled by colour schemes and furniture (good or bad) — you can always repaint and the furniture will be replaced with your own. You will also want to:

- *Turn on taps.* Turn them all on, even the shower — this will allow you to check the water pressure.

- *Check the toilet.* Flush it to check it works and doesn't shake up the whole plumbing system in the process. Look for any leaks and cracks.

- *Inspect the walls and ceilings.* This means looking for cracks and dips. A dipping ceiling could mean there's a water leak in the roof. Black spots might suggest dampness. Cracks around cornices often indicate structural movement, whereas cracks around doors and windows are usually not as serious.

- *Look at wet areas.* Look out for rotting timber under and around the unit's wet areas (kitchen, bathroom, toilet, laundry). A leaky shower could affect wall frame timbers.

- *Check all windows.* Curtains and blinds do a great job of hiding little imperfections. Figure 3.1 shows a rotting window sash that is barely holding the window pane in place. Check that there are no cracks in the windows and that they open and close easily. While you're there, see if they have locks (this makes a difference to your insurance).

Figure 3.1: a loose window pane that could fall on a passer-by below

Photo by Stephen Raff

☞ *Turn off the lights.* Often when you inspect a property the real estate agent has turned on all the lights to make it appear brighter, even in the middle of the day. Go around and switch off all the lights and compare the difference. You don't want to find yourself living in a dungeon with no natural light!

Outside, there are also a number of things to look out for:

☞ *Large cracks.* Larger cracks that follow the course of the brickwork are serious and may indicate that the problem will have to be solved by underpinning the corner of the building and/or by constructing a retaining wall (see figures 3.2 and 3.3, overleaf). These solutions can become very expensive.

Figure 3.2: patched-up structural damage

Photo by Stephen Raff

Figure 3.3: a cracked wall that could be the result of normal ground movement or a major structural defect

Photo by Stephen Raff

☞ *Gardens close to the unit.* Watering gardens that are close to the perimeter can cause structural problems with the foundations. Alternatively, a unit that is surrounded by concrete can be a concern; a lack of water can allow the foundations to dry out and shift.

- *Ground level.* If the external ground is higher or equal to the internal floor level, check that there is adequate drainage to avoid flooding.

- *Vents.* Make sure gardens do not cover vents on the outside of a unit. This can lead to internal mildew attack.

- *Large trees close by.* Check for large trees that are within two metres of the unit. Tree roots can often cause cracking of walls and driveways (see figure 3.4), which is an occupational health and safety risk. The cost of replacing them will come out of your fees.

Figure 3.4: a cracked concrete driveway

Photo by Stephen Raff

- *Guttering and downpipes.* If guttering and downpipes are not connected properly it could lead to severe cracking and damp spots within the unit.

- *Rising damp and mildew.* Look for evidence of rising damp to the brickwork areas below floor level and external to the property. Look for mildew growth at the base of the brickwork on external walls and also flaking paintwork.

☛ *Leaning walls.* Walls with a visible lean (as shown in figure 3.5) can potentially collapse, causing untold damage to people and property.

Figure 3.5: a leaning wall

Photo by Stephen Raff

With any damage you find, don't necessarily believe agents if they respond to your queries with a cursory 'the body corporate will fix that'. That might not actually be right, or it might not be such an easy process. Ask if the current owners will fix anything you're really concerned about before you settle (this is also a possible request before an auction — more about that in chapter 4).

Case study: buyer beware

Brent Catoggio, a high-profile AFL footballer, bought an eight-year-old premium townhouse in the Melbourne suburb of North Carlton, overlooking Princes Park. He had checked it out on the internet but with football commitments interstate, didn't have the chance to inspect the property himself. He sent his mother to have a look instead, and she assured him it was a great buy.

When the time came to move in, Brent noticed some rust spots appearing in the render. It worried him so he had the place inspected by a qualified building surveyor.

The surveyor found evidence of major rust behind the building's walls that was compromising the integrity of the structure, making it unstable and dangerous. One quote to repair it came in at six figures.

Brent took his case against the townhouse's builder to the Victorian Civil and Administrative Tribunal but lost, the tribunal noting the provisions of 'buyer beware'. The tribunal ruled that had Brent inspected the property himself he would have noticed the spots that were found to be clearly evident at the time of purchase.

Professional building inspections

If you're not confident about spotting all these potential faults yourself, you can always organise a pre-purchase inspection by an architect or registered builder. In fact, unless you are an engineer, I'd recommend you get an inspection anyway — there's too much at risk for you to pretend you are your best adviser. There are many of these services available and they usually provide you with a comprehensive report of the property that considers structural damage, dampness, timber pest damage, defective plumbing, shoddy construction and other defects. The builder/architect will usually inspect around the grounds, under the floor, into the roof and all through the unit, reporting on any visible faults.

To find a building inspection service in your area, simply do an internet search for 'building inspections' or check your local yellow pages. Archicentre (the building advisory service of the Royal Australian Institute of Architects) also provides home inspection reports Australia wide <www.archicentre.com.au>.

At the very least get a friend (preferably someone who knows something about buildings) to come and have a look with you.

A note on doing detective work

These are just things to consider. If a unit is otherwise perfect for you, you're not going to pass it up just because the water pressure is not as strong as you're used to. However, being aware of these things helps to avoid disappointment after you move in. Another advantage is that some of the more serious defects or issues you find may become a bargaining chip when negotiating a selling price with the vendor.

Case study: cracking up

Madeleine and Ben ran a keen eye over every inch of the unit they planned to buy for their parents' retirement. It was a relatively new place, they thought, and on the surface it all looked perfect except for a minor hairline crack in the dining room. Friends assured them it was no big deal. Someone told Ben if you couldn't fit a match-head into the crack, it wasn't worth worrying about. So he didn't.

Madeleine and Ben bought the unit through private sale and submitted their deposit. A few days before settlement they were invited to do a final inspection. During that inspection, Madeleine noticed a water stain in the dining room ceiling and started to become concerned. She quickly called a building consultant to inspect the damage and try to determine a cause.

According to the consultant, water had seeped through the roof because the unit had settled since its construction and that meant movement. That settling also explained the hairline crack they noticed when they first viewed the property. Delving further, Madeleine and Ben discovered that the unit had been built on pre-existing bluestone foundations that were over 100 years old. They were advised to get a structural engineer to investigate the issue properly.

The engineer found that the foundations were inadequate and major structural works would be required to ensure that the unit no longer shifted excessively. The costs, they discovered, would be more than double their initial deposit.

What exactly are you buying?

Another thing you'll want to have crystal clear in your mind (and in the contract of sale!) is the division of your property and common property (refer back to the list of vendor disclosure documents in table 2.2).

When most people think of common property, they usually think of the obvious aspects: the shared driveways that run between townhouses, hallways in blocks of flats, lifts in high-rise apartments. These are usually pretty safe assumptions, but there are many others to consider such as windows, doors, balconies, fences and awnings where definitions tend to differ from state to state. As you will come to discover throughout this book, it is important to understand exactly what you are buying (that is, what's yours and what's shared) before signing on the dotted line. This will mean careful scrutiny of your contract of sale (and consulting a property lawyer if necessary), but there are also a number of state-specific laws and regulations that you should be aware of that may not be specified in your individual contract. See appendix A for a state-by-state summary of some of these laws and regulations.

Generally speaking, all internal parts of your unit (the surfaces of the walls, floors, ceilings, the inside of window frames and doors) are yours to do whatever you wish with. All external parts (outside walls, roofs, the external side of windows and doors) belong to the body corporate. (This isn't always the case. See appendix A for a more detailed state-by-state breakdown.)

So, while you are allowed to paint the inside of your front door, you usually can't touch the outside. Internal blinds? Fine. External? Off limits. The upside of this is that the body corporate is usually responsible for any maintenance and repairs to these external areas. The downside is that you may not like the colour of the external side of your front door or the executive committee may be slower than you'd like at organising repairs.

If you want to make structural changes to the inside of your unit, such as pulling down a wall between a lounge and dining room to open up the space, this will usually have to go through the committee and may eventually require a special or unanimous resolution of the body corporate, particularly if you live in an apartment block where the walls you wish to level may be weight-bearing and affect the other homes above you.

Builder's warranty insurance

If you do find yourself in a situation after you've bought a unit where things are falling down around you (providing it is a relatively new unit), all states have builder's warranty insurance. But be careful: it is time-limited, as shown in table 3.1.

Table 3.1: time limits on builder's warranty insurance, by region

Region	Time limit
ACT	Five years from certificate of occupancy date
NSW	For structural defects six years from the time the defects are noticed by the owners. For non-structural defects the time limit is two years.
NT	There is no statutory obligation; however, the builders give varying periods of warranty from 13 weeks up to 2 years[#]
Qld	Time limits for making a claim are six years and three months for category 1 defects and six months for category 2 defects[*]
SA	Five years from the completion date
Tas.	Six years from the completion date
Vic.	Structural defects are six years and non-structural defects are two years. However, time limits in Victoria start from the date the contract is completed
WA	Six years from the completion date

[*] Home warranty insurance in Queensland is underwritten by the government; there are no private insurers. The procedure in Queensland involves making a claim on the insurer first, rather than having to go through the builder as in other states.

[#] The Northern Territory Government operates an insurance provider called Territory Insurance Office (TIO). Other providers may also be used.

In both New South Wales and Victoria, the claim can be made on a builder's warranty insurance only where the builder can't be found, is deceased or insolvent/ceased trading.

In most states and territories, the builder is exempt from having compulsory warranty insurance in multistorey residential buildings. The definition of multistorey varies slightly from state to state, but in most cases it will exclude a building that has over three storeys.

It's important to remember though that, due to the multistorey exemption now in force in most states and territories (excluding South Australia and the ACT), prospective unit owners need to ensure that the builder is a reputable one before purchasing a property in a building over three storeys high. There is no home warranty cover for strata buildings over three storeys high in Victoria, New South Wales, Northern Territory and Western Australia.

Buyers should also make sure to take immediate action after noticing any defect. Identifying defects and making a claim against a builder or an insurer can be a long and costly exercise and should be dealt with sooner rather than later with the help of professional legal advice.

Need more help looking into a particular property?

Some of these people might be able to help with your inspections:

- *Body corporate manager*. These companies can give local advice and help you interpret plans so you understand what will belong to you and what is common property.

- *Body corporate committee chairperson*. If you can access a member of the body corporate's committee you may be able to get the inside running on upcoming plans for the scheme.

- *Lawyers and solicitors*. Property lawyers will be able to advise on legal issues associated with strata schemes and their plans of subdivision.

- *State/territory-based fair trading office*. These government organisations often produce information (both online and in print) about buying into strata properties.

- *Body corporate agencies/consultants.* Some are specifically set up to investigate pre-purchase information on the owners' behalf.

- *Real estate agents and agencies.* Agents can help you understand the local market better.

- *Property inspectors, building engineers and surveyors.* For information about what might be lurking behind those beautifully painted walls and lush carpets.

- *Accountants.* Accountants can help you decipher financial statements.

From my experience of running a business in strata properties, I'm still surprised by how little some of these professionals know about the issues of living or buying a strata unit. Don't just go to any expert, go to one experienced in strata properties.

What next?

Now that you're satisfied you know more about the physical state of the property you're interested in, the next chapter looks at the different ways property is sold in today's market — and the pros and cons of each.

Chapter 4

Ways to buy

Once upon a time there was really only one way to buy a property: private sale/treaty. It all seemed so simple: the existing owner or developer would advertise a too-high price, interested buyers would offer something lower, negotiate from there and you would eventually agree on a figure. Then auctions came along. Originally used for legal reasons when will executors or foreclosing banks had to sell off a property in a public and transparent way, auctions have gained popularity among real estate agents who convince their clients that it is the best way to get the maximum price for their property. Excited buyers huddle around an auctioneer, get caught up in the hype and excitement of a live bidding war and drive the price up and up until the auctioneer calls 'Going once, going twice, for the third and final call ... SOLD!'

Private sales are still popular all over Australia and the decision to go for an auction or private sale is made between the real estate agent and the seller, based on the usual practice in the sale area, the type of property for sale and the market trend at the time. Buyers don't get a choice (except of course if you make an offer before auction). But now there are even more options available to sellers, as you will see in the list of current sale methods listed below.

Private sale/treaty

As I mentioned, buying a unit through a private sale or private treaty is as straightforward as the seller listing the property with the agent, the agent advertising it at an agreed (although always inflated) price, and showing prospective buyers through at scheduled times. Interested parties make offers through the agent (usually starting significantly lower than the advertised price) and the seller settles with what they think will be the best offer they'll get.

One tip when buying your unit via a private sale: attach an expiry date to your offer (a 'sunset clause') to limit the seller's ability to drag out negotiations or sit on your offer indefinitely while they negotiate with others. But make it a reasonable amount of time — five to seven working days is enough.

Auction

As daunting as auctions can be, unfortunately it's not up to you to decide whether the place you want is being offered for sale in this way. You may not be able to avoid it. If you don't think you have the nerve to bid on a property (or think you will get too excited and not stop bidding until you win, despite the fact you may not be able to afford it), it's wise to get someone else to bid for you. The advantage of having an impartial third party means that they will stick to your instructions to the letter and not let emotions get in the way of their bidding. This person might be a trusted relative, a friend, a solicitor or even a buyer's advocate (a professional who helps you source and buy a property, and who is usually paid a part of the purchase price).

If you decide to go this way, and choose to not attend the auction at all, it might also be an idea to be easily available on the phone or to stay on the line while the auction is in progress, just in case you need to communicate with your representative. Buyers sometimes go this route if they feel as if they have given too much away to the selling agent about their price limit or interest in the property.

If you are going to bid yourself and you haven't much experience with auctions, it's a good idea to go along to a few and see how they work. It's especially good to go along to other auctions run by the agent who is selling the property you're interested in so you become familiar with their style.

Although you are pretty much locked into the sale if you are the last person standing at the end of the auction, there are things you can negotiate. It is best to do this with the selling agent before auction day and might include aspects such as the settlement period and the size of your deposit. So, you might say to the agent beforehand: 'If I am the successful bidder, I want it to be a 60- or 90-day settlement'. Or, 'If I am the successful bidder, I want to be able to settle on 19 October'. Or, 'If I am the successful bidder, I only want to pay a five per cent deposit on the day, with another five per cent payable after 30 days and the balance on settlement'. Anything can be arranged. No request is off the table. If you have a special need, ask. It can't hurt. Maybe you will stipulate that you want the windows professionally cleaned or an existing cubby house in the backyard removed.

Case study: pre-auction offers

It seemed Diana and Dennis had been looking for their ideal next home forever. For countless weekends they trawled through the internet, leafed through the real estate pages of their local newspaper, spoke with real estate agents and visited properties.

Case study: pre-auction offers (cont'd)

With a baby on the way, their one-bedroom unit was going to get very small very quickly. Its inner-city location, they decided, wasn't going to be an ideal place to raise a child. They wanted to be closer to kindergartens, parks and other young families.

Finally, they found exactly what they were looking for. Instantly, they fell in love with a three-bedroom townhouse in a leafy suburb only 12 kilometres from the city. Located on a quiet street, there were three parks close-by, walking tracks, kids' play equipment and even a man-made lake with some ducks. Great kindergartens and schools were within walking distance and a doctor's surgery was located just up the road.

As they should, both Diana and Dennis perused the vendor statement that was available through the agent. They had spoken with their bank and knew they had approval to bid up to a figure they hoped would secure them the property. The only thing left to do was to wait for auction day.

That day finally came. But as they drove up the street to their dream home their excitement soon turned to horror. Plastered across the 'for sale' sign were four letters that ended it all: SOLD.

What went wrong?

Pre-auction offers

Pre-auction offers are a reality of selling property this way. Even though the vendor has advertised an auction date, there is nothing stopping them from selling beforehand if they get a good enough offer — and one they don't think they'll top at auction.

The best way to avoid losing out on a unit this way is to clearly register your interest with the selling agent. Ask if they will consider pre-auction offers. If the answer is yes, make one. But make it low. That way, they know to come back to you if they get another offer that is closer to the mark.

Tips for buying at auction

- Have a strategy beforehand.
- Check the contract of sale again on auction day to make sure nothing has changed.
- Bid clearly and confidently.
- Stick to your limit.
- Under no circumstances reveal your maximum price to anyone representing the selling agent.
- Ask someone else to bid if you don't feel confident—this removes all emotion.

Dummy bidding

Dummy bids are fake bids made at an auction by attendees with no real intent to buy the property. These bids are placed in an attempt to artificially inflate the price of a property, usually to mislead or deceive potential buyers. Dummy bidding used to happen in two ways: either the auctioneer pretended to take a bid from someone in the crowd, when, in reality, no real person made the bid; or the real estate agent planted 'stooges' in the crowd to submit false bids.

Dummy bidding has been going on for as long as auctions have. The real estate industry has long denied that it happens as a sanctioned part of their selling process; however, there is no question that the practice has been widespread. Officially, 'dummy bidding' is being outlawed in all Australian states and territories. What has been introduced in its place is 'vendor bids', which are bids that the auctioneer declares as such, usually to get slow auctions moving. Table 4.1 outlines the laws related to dummy bidding across Australia.

Table 4.1: dummy bidding legislation around Australia

Region	Dummy bidding law
ACT	Dummy bidding will be outlawed under proposed new laws, and one vendor bid will be allowed at auction.
NSW	The law was clarified in 2007 to say that dummy bidding at auctions is now an explicit offence, with a maximum penalty of $55 000. The single vendor bid can now be made only by the auctioneer, who, prior to the auction, needs to announce the vendor bid restrictions and dummy bidding prohibition. All bidders must register before auction.
NT	The Territory government is reviewing the *Auctioneers Act*.
Qld	Dummy bids were outlawed in 2006 with bidders having to register prior to bidding and auctioneers required to acknowledge vendor bids.
SA	It is an offence for anyone to make or procure a dummy bid as well as for an auctioneer to knowingly take or procure a dummy bid.
Tas.	The state government plans to introduce legislation to ban dummy bidding and for vendor bidding to face more disclosure.
Vic.	Dummy bidding is prohibited, but 'permissible vendors' bids' are allowed, that is, bids that are declared as vendor bids.
WA	Dummy bidding is not outlawed; however, the Real Estate Institute of Western Australia has amended its code of conduct to ban the practice of agents pitting dummy bidders against genuine home buyers.

Sale by tender

Selling by tender is another option open to sellers. Although not very widespread, it involves putting the property on the market at an unstipulated price and calling for offers to be submitted in writing prior to a specified future date. All offers are then considered, one of which may be accepted and the property sold.

Self-selling

Fed up with real estate agents taking two to three per cent commission on the sale and paying high marketing costs, some buyers are opting to do it all themselves. With online shopping becoming more and more popular, some sellers have taken to marketing and selling their properties themselves with the help of a conveyancer or property lawyer to assist with the legal paperwork. This method of sale is now used in up to about 40 per cent of property sales in the United States and Britain, so it's popularity here will no doubt only grow.

There is lots of help out there for self-sellers. For buyers, here's where you can start your search:

- eBay <www.ebay.com.au>
- *Trading Post* <www.tradingpost.com.au>
- Property Post <www.propertypost.com.au>
- dwelling.com.au <www.dwelling.com.au>
- BuyItPrivately.com.au <www.buyitprivately.com.au>
- U Sell Property <www.usellproperty.com>
- Self Sell Home Sales <www.selfsellhomesales.com.au> (WA only).

As a buyer, I can understand why you might be wary of a property being sold this way, but, in reality, assuming the paperwork is in order, you are no more exposed than if you bought through an agent. As in all cases, it might be wise (and for your peace of mind) to organise a professional building inspection to identify any structural faults or other defects (see chapter 3). Table 4.2 outlines the pros and cons of each method of buying property.

Table 4.2: pros and cons of different buying methods

Buying method	Pros	Cons
Auction	You know you're getting the price at market value. Often flexibility to negotiate the settlement date. Designed to be an open and transparent process.	Emotions can take over in the heat of battle and you might end up spending more than you budgeted for. No cooling-off period if you change your mind after a restless night's sleep. All reports and inspections must be done before bidding, with no guarantee of a successful bid. You must pay the full deposit immediately (unless a prior arrangement has been made).

Buying method	Pros	Cons
Private sale	Cooling-off period. You know the asking price. More opportunity to negotiate the contract conditions than at auction. You can complete all reports and inspections before the end of the cooling-off period (if there is one) and withdraw your offer if anything is wrong.	You don't know what price the seller will accept. You might pay too much for a property; you don't know if what you're paying is market value. More room for negotiation.
Tender	More time to consider what you will offer. Less chance of exceeding your budget on a whim.	Only get one opportunity to submit an offer.
Self-selling	May save money since the owner won't have to pay agent's commissions. May not be competing against as many buyers.	These properties may be harder to find. The paperwork will need to be scrutinised even more closely.

There are whole books dedicated to buying property. I have only really gone over the basics here.

Buying off the plan

Let's face it: property developers do a pretty slick job of marketing strata properties off the plan. If the glossy brochures aren't enough to get you in, the display apartment spirits away any lingering doubts. The kitchen is gleaming, the walls and floor are mark-free and the furniture is modern and immaculate. Of course you give a fleeting thought to how your existing furniture might fit in the place, but then the salesperson begins a spiel featuring gorgeous views, a pool, spa and gym.

And then there are the financial benefits: no stamp duty to pay and the promise of a handsome increase in value the moment the key is handed over.

Case study: the fine print

Danielle, a divorcee with three young children, looked at buying off the plan as a way of making her half of the value of the former family home go further. Her plan was to move in with her parents while her strata property was built—another way to save money until her place was built.

The display unit impressed her and its price suited her budget. Danielle was surprised at the quality she could get through buying off the plan.

When it came time to choose her fixtures and fittings, Danielle realised why the display unit looked so good and the price seemed so attractive—everything in the display suite was top of the range and everything she had chosen (in line with the advertised price) was at the bottom. Although everything looked fine in the brochures, Danielle began to worry.

After two proposed completion dates had passed, Danielle finally moved into her brand new unit with her three children. But it was not what she expected. Somehow it didn't look quite as good as

---

the display unit. The kitchen, while gleaming, lacked class. Where was the granite benchtop? The cheaper laminate 'timber' flooring she'd chosen wasn't half as impressive as the genuine timber featured in the display unit. And the bathroom? She didn't want to discuss it.

Thankfully, with a little homework and the right advice, this situation can be avoided. Figure 4.1 shows an off-the-plan development in construction.

Figure 4.1: buying off the plan has its pros and cons

Photo by Matt Davies

Investigate the developer

This is often easier said than done with variability in quality affecting even the best regarded developers. The first thing to do is to check other properties they've developed. If you have the gumption, talk to residents about how well their home has stood the test of time and talk to the building and strata managers about any problems they may have encountered.

Another avenue for advice is your state-based consumer affairs agency or Office of Fair Trading (see appendix D for helpful references). They will be able to tell you if any complaints have been levelled against a particular developer and what, if any, investigations are underway or have been completed.

The other difficulty is that it is not uncommon for smaller or newer companies to go into liquidation halfway through a project (only to set up shop again under a new name) and to have the construction taken over by another builder. Sometimes developers subcontract construction to other companies or sell off the contract before the job is complete. The first things to suffer in these circumstances are the finishing touches—all those details that make one property stand out from another. This also makes it difficult to rectify problems that might emerge after you've moved in. One builder will invariably blame another, and even going down the path of initiating legal action may not solve your problems. In fact, it may create even more. It's a much better approach to check the reputation and history of your builder. Those companies that have been in business longer are always going to be a safer bet.

Have your contract looked over by a lawyer before you sign. Highlight anything you don't understand and ask the lawyer to explain it to you. All inclusions or exclusions, such as a specific type of heating or security system will be noted in the contract. Make sure they are there as you understand them. It might also be helpful to make your own list based on what the developer has verbally promised and to check them off as you go through the contract. Ascertain if there's a penalty for withdrawing from the contract and, if construction finishes ahead of schedule, that your finance will be available. A lawyer should also ensure that the contract includes:

- a 'sunset clause' (in other words, it becomes null and void if the development is not completed by a certain date)

- a condition that variance in floor area will not exceed a prescribed maximum (a small degree of variance is quite common).

Others areas to look out for when buying off the plan include:

- Have there been any community objections to the building that may lead to a change in the design?

- Has the development actually been approved by local council (again, this could dramatically affect the final design, including the removal of some of the key features such as a tennis court).

- Unless stated in the contract, ask what happens with your deposit in the event that the developer goes bust or the building isn't finished on time. You don't want to leave them with your deposit if they end up running two years behind schedule! If possible, negotiate to provide a deposit bond upon signing, rather than a deposit.

- As with any strata property, check the fees. The joy of moving in to your new property will soon disappear if you're hit with an exorbitant bill for strata fees that you didn't expect (more about fees in chapter 6).

Finally, all these things I've suggested you check — get them in writing. That might be in the form of a letter, an email or even a piece of paper on which you write down the details and ask the developer to sign.

One last piece of advice when buying off the plan: get a final building inspection done by a qualified consultant *before* you pay the balance of the purchase price.

What next?

Now that you've bought and moved into your strata property, what are your responsibilities to the body corporate? What are its responsibilities to you? Chapter 5 investigates these matters.

Responsibilities of bodies corporate... and owners

To recap, a body corporate is simply the group of unit owners in a strata scheme. How many times have I heard people talk as if the body corporate was some kind of Santa Claus with a bucketful of cash! When you own a strata unit, the body corporate is you and your fellow owners. They make by-laws/rules and have many responsibilities to the unit owners, but, as outlined in previous chapters, owners do have responsibilities when living in a strata property situation.

A body corporate comes into existence when its strata plan is registered with the state-based land titles authority.

Exceptions

In some states (including Victoria and Western Australia) two-lot subdivisions are exempt from many requirements such as notices of fees, procedures for meetings and decision making, keeping records and a body corporate register, and taking out insurance in the name of the body corporate.

In Victoria, for example, prescribed owners corporations have additional requirements they need to meet. Prescribed bodies corporate are those that have more than 100 units or collect more than $200 000 in fees per year. They also need to:

⊷ establish a maintenance plan

⊷ have financial statements audited every year

⊷ obtain a building valuation every five years.

Obligations

The main obligations of bodies corporate (you and your fellow owners) are to:

⊷ manage and administer the common property

⊷ repair and maintain the common property, fixtures and services

⊷ take out and maintain required insurance, including building insurance and common property liability insurance

⊷ collect and manage fees from unit owners

⊷ keep financial records, including preparing financial statements

⊷ provide a grievance/dispute procedure for dealing with complaints and other issues

⊷ adhere to legal obligations as outlined in their state or territory's strata legislation (for a list of each state's legislation see chapter 1).

Record keeping

Bodies corporate are required to keep records as prescribed by their state or territory legislation as well as by federal requirements, such as taxation laws. All voting papers and ballots should be kept and in some states must be kept for at least 12 months following the vote. Proxies should be kept and in some states must also be retained for 12 months after they expire or are revoked. Table 5.1 (overleaf) outlines the length of time records must be kept for each state and territory.

Generally, bodies corporate are required to keep:

- a copy of the strata plan (also known by other names depending on which state or territory you are in — see glossary)
- a copy of the body corporate rules/by-laws
- details of unit owners (including full names and addresses)
- minutes of committee and general meetings
- copies of any resolutions reached
- records of the results of ballots
- proxies
- voting papers
- copies of all correspondence sent and received (for at least seven years)
- accounting records, tax returns (including any GST records) and other financial statements (see chapter 6 for more on fees and financial management)
- insurance policies
- maintenance plans (if applicable)
- any legal documents served on the body corporate such as notices or orders
- signed contracts and agreements with suppliers

↪ leases and licences over common property* (such as telephone towers, signage, leasing of car spots, land and storage units).

* Note: If the body corporate leases out any common property then that income is deposited into the body corporate's account. The income is distributed among the members based on unit entitlement and needs to be added to the unit owner's taxable income. This requirement can vary from state to state so professional tax advice is recommended.

Table 5.1: length of time records must be stored, by region

Region	Years accounts kept for	Years minutes kept for	Exemptions for small schemes?
ACT	5	5	–
NSW	5	5	Yes
NT	3	3	–
Qld	6	Life of scheme	–
SA	7	30	Yes
Tas.	N/A	N/A	–
Vic.	7	7	Yes
WA	7	7	Yes

Insurance

It is the responsibility of the body corporate to take out certain insurance with approved insurers to cover the strata scheme. The cost of this is covered in fees paid into the body corporate by unit owners.

You will need to carefully research what each policy is offering. Insurance covers can vary substantially from company to company. Some of the included cover will not be available with some insurance polices. There are specialist insurance companies that you can consult to ensure you and your body corporate are getting adequate protection.

Building and common area contents

This type of insurance covers properties against accidental loss or damage up to a specified sum. A damage policy should cover damage from fire, lightning, an explosion, storm, flood, earthquake, aircraft, riot and civil commotion, malicious damage (including that caused by a tenant), vehicle impact, theft, vandalism, glass breakage, or anything else that might result in a building needing to be replaced or restored to its original condition. This should include removal of any debris that has been created through the damage and any costs of engaging architects or other service contractors to complete the work.

The 'building' is usually considered to include all fixtures and fittings such as internal doors, cupboards, stoves, sinks, toilet bowls, shower screens, light fittings and hot water systems and shared fittings in common areas, electronic security systems and air-conditioning systems. The policy should also cover accidental breakage and any other event that is not specifically excluded (such as flood, wear and tear, corrosion and vermin).

Other insurances that should be considered for a strata scheme are:

- *Public/legal liability insurance.* Covers any property damage, injury or death for which the body corporate may be responsible. Legislation in some states sets minimum indemnities (generally $10 million), but in view of increasing awards made by courts, higher indemnities should be considered.

- *Office bearers liability insurance.* This insurance is designed to provide indemnity for officers carrying out their duties and obligations in managing a body corporate should they become legally liable to pay compensation for a wrongful act. This can include committee members, a managing agent appointed as an office bearer or someone who is invited by an office bearer to assist in managing the body corporate's affairs.

- *Workers compensation insurance.* Covers staff hired by the body corporate under state-based workers compensation legislation. By law, insurance companies are not permitted to issue workers compensation cover in Queensland, Victoria or South Australia. (Workers compensation insurance is discussed later in this chapter.)

- *Voluntary workers insurance.* Covers volunteers (someone who works without accepting a fee or other reward) who might work around the property on behalf of the body corporate. Benefits usually apply to anyone over 12 years old.

- *Fidelity guarantee.* This protects against losses resulting from the dishonesty of employees, such as misappropriation of body corporate funds or property.

- *Machinery breakdown.* Provides protection against unforeseen damage to electrical, electronic and mechanical machinery including elevators, escalators and incliners (assuming they are subject to a valid maintenance agreement).

- *Catastrophe insurance.* Provides protection against a sudden escalation in building costs that results from a catastrophe such as an earthquake or cyclone; it also often applies to other loss that occurs to insured property not more than 60 days after the event.

✦ *Government audit costs.* This type of insurance can cover costs associated with a tax office (or other statutory body) investigation or a record-keeping audit by a business affairs authority. It might also cover legal expenses incurred in appealing against an improvement or prohibition notice brought under workplace, occupational health, safety or similar legislation.

✦ *Legal defence expenses.* Covers costs of defending an action against the body corporate (or where the body corporate is joined in litigation with another party).

✦ *Unit owners' fixtures and improvements.* This provides additional cover against accidental loss or damage to improvements made by unit owners that may not have been included in the body corporate building valuation.

Please be aware that this information is only a guide. It is strongly recommend that you consult a specialist insurer to ensure you have the required insurance cover for your body corporate and unit owners.

Legislative requirements

State governments have introduced legislation that imposes obligations on bodies corporate to insure the building for its full reinstatement or replacement value, as shown in table 5.2 (overleaf). However, the Acts do not define replacement value, which can vary enormously depending on the specific circumstances of the loss, such as when individual owners have made upgrades to their units. On top of that, owners may find they can't rebuild their unit according to its original structure because the council may have imposed laws restricting the building heights in the area since it was originally built.

Table 5.2: insurance obligations under legislation, by region

Region	Required insurance	Inclusions
ACT	Building replacement Liability	Building Common property Owners' fixtures (indirectly)
NSW	Building replacement Liability	Building Common property Owners' fixtures
Qld	Building replacement Liability	Building Common property Owners' fixtures
SA	Building replacement Liability	Building Common property
Tas.	Building replacement and reinstatement insurance Public risk insurance	Building Common property Owners' fixtures
Vic.	Rebuild/reconstruct Public liability	Building*, including improvements and unit owners' fixtures Common property
WA	Rebuild/reconstruct Liability	Building Common property Owners' fixtures

* Building valuations are mandatory for prescribed owners corporations.

Note: In the Northern Territory insurance can be provided by the government. With a high risk of cyclone damage, some private companies are reluctant to provide cover.

Given these anomalies, when you are investigating whether or not the insurance cover is adequate, you may want to consider the following:

- *Environmental hazards.* Are there any environmentally hazardous materials on or near the property or contained in the soils that would prevent rebuilding?

- *Planning restrictions.* Planning laws often change. Laws that have come into effect since the building was originally constructed may prevent the same building being constructed on the site. In some cases, a badly damaged building (rather than one that is completely destroyed) may even be refused reinstatement.

- *Minimum distances.* The building being less than the minimum distance from, say, adjoining bushland under bushfire regulations may prevent a building being reconstructed.

- *Local objections.* Consider whether locals would be likely to object to the building if it were a new construction. Also consider Aboriginal land issues; local tribes could object because of sacred sites.

- *Dangerous materials.* Under occupational health and safety laws, the existence of hazard materials such as asbestos, lead dust or deteriorated fibreglass insulation may need to be professionally removed before work can begin at a damage site. This will cost extra and may not be covered.

- *GST.* Some bodies corporate discount the sum insured on the building to exclude the GST component in the belief that it is fully recoverable or never payable. Consequently, you need to include the GST component when determining your insured sum. Whether a body corporate is registered for GST will affect the amount it will receive under an insurance claim.

꒑ *Building valuations.* In addition to any legislative requirements, insurance companies recommend that bodies corporate engage a professional building valuer to value the property every three to five years to ensure cover is still adequate.

Note that in South Australia buildings can be insured individually by owners. However, it's recommended that they are insured as a group. This allows for greater consistency of cover, can make claims easier and can be more cost effective.

Delegation of power

In a body corporate situation, voting rights are allocated according to number of units, not number of individuals. Therefore, if one person owns four units, for example, they are entitled to four votes (except in the ACT where there is a maximum of one). It also means that if a unit is jointly owned, the owners are only able to submit one collective vote. There is no limit on proxies that can be held by one member.

Bodies corporate generally have a hierarchy of power, as illustrated in figure 5.1.

Strata managers

In some strata schemes, usually those with three or more units, the body corporate may elect to appoint a strata manager (also called a body corporate manager or owners corporation manager) or a managing agent to carry out some or all of their duties. The decision to appoint a manager or managing agent must be made by a majority vote of the body corporate, with the length of time of that appointment being decided in the same way.

Figure 5.1: hierarchy of power in a body corporate*

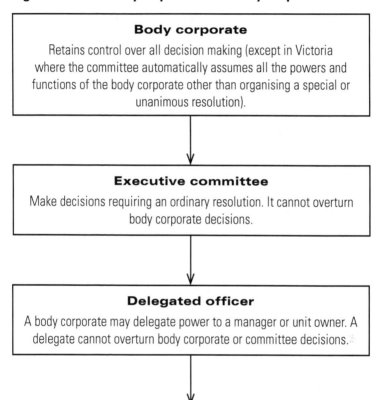

Body corporate
Retains control over all decision making (except in Victoria where the committee automatically assumes all the powers and functions of the body corporate other than organising a special or unanimous resolution).

Executive committee
Make decisions requiring an ordinary resolution. It cannot overturn body corporate decisions.

Delegated officer
A body corporate may delegate power to a manager or unit owner. A delegate cannot overturn body corporate or committee decisions.

Subcommittees
Bodies corporate sometimes appoint subcommittees to provide advice. Subcommittees can make recommendations and, in some states and territories, the full powers of the body corporate can be delegated to a subcommittee.

* This may vary slightly from state to state.

A strata manager or managing agent performs only the tasks stipulated by the body corporate, which are usually outlined in the management agreement. The managing agent will often take care of the following details:

- Providing continuity of management processes and record keeping for the body corporate. Problems can arise with frequent changes in voluntary members who undertake the management duties, resulting in different standards of record keeping and potentially inadequate or missing records. Employing a managing agent can help to alleviate this problem.

- Ensuring taxation and legislative matters are being adhered to, submitting tax returns for the body corporate, if necessary, and GST/BAS statement processing/preparation.

- Resolving disputes and providing an objective approach to dealing with members' concerns or disputes. Disputes are reasonably common and tend to be issues such as parking, noise, pets, adjacent developments and so on. An objective, professional committee or body corporate manager can assist in these situations, as can external bodies and authorities if the dispute escalates.

- Looking after body corporate administration and handling day-to-day paperwork and requests from solicitors, etc. The manager often organises annual and special/extraordinary general meetings including minutes, facilitates setting of budgets, collects members' contributions and maintains a complete set of financial statements.

- Coordinating the issuing of leases and licences on behalf of the body corporate where necessary.

- Administering insurance, dealing with brokers and directly with insurance companies as necessary. This might include submitting claims, scheduling repair work, obtaining quotes and processing claims paperwork. They can also provide general and factual advice and options to members (if they are an authorised representative of the insurance company) in relation to all body corporate insurance issues.

- Coordinating the maintenance of body corporate facilities and essential services including obtaining quotes and scheduling work as required, ensuring that the strata scheme is maintained in good condition and presents no dangers to visitors or members. They can also schedule essential services reports as necessary and review compliance with current legislation.

- Scheduling grounds maintenance and liaising with caretakers, gardeners and tradespeople to ensure that grounds are maintained to members' requirements.

While a manager/managing agent is appointed to perform the general functions of the body corporate as outlined above (or at least the ones stipulated in their contract), managers/agents cannot:

- make a decision on a restricted matter

- set levies

- delegate their powers to others.

If the body corporate is not satisfied with the manager/ managing agent's performance, they should write a letter in the first instance, outlining their concerns. Failing that, a meeting should be arranged to talk through the issues in line with whatever dispute resolution process has been stipulated in the contract. As a last resort, the body corporate can cancel the contract with a majority vote (or according to the terms laid out in the contract).

Not all states have a requirement that body corporate managers need to be licensed or even carry professional indemnity insurance (see table 5.3), but some benefits of employing a manager are that:

- it saves body corporate members' time dealing with day-to-day issues they may not have expertise in

- managers keep up to date with relevant legalisation and reporting requirements

- members have access to specialist contractors and tradespeople for the strata sector and other resources not publicly available to self-managed bodies corporate.

Table 5.3: qualifications of managers, by region

Region	Must managers be licensed?	Must managers have professional indemnity insurance?
ACT	✓	✗
NSW	✓	✓
NT	✓	✓
Qld	✗	✗
SA	✗	✗
Tas.	✗	✗
Vic.	✗*	✓
WA	✗	✗

* Although Victorian strata mangers don't need to be licensed they do need to be registered with the Business Licensing Authority.

Caretakers and building managers

Larger bodies corporate may also elect to appoint a building manager or caretaker to help them fulfil their duties. Building managers don't have the same power as a managing agent, but they might assist the body corporate with managing common property, including overseeing maintenance.

A building manager is usually appointed at the first AGM. If the original owner of the strata scheme had a building manager in place already, this contract may terminate at the first AGM depending on the original contract. The AGM or executive committee will then decide whether or not they need a building manager and the functions that the manager should perform. They may even opt to transfer the contract with the original owner to the new body corporate if they are happy with past performance.

Delegation of the body corporate's powers, by region

Australian Capital Territory—may engage people, such as a professional managing agent, to assist in carrying out its functions. Managers are not required to be licensed.

New South Wales—can appoint a manager/managing agent to assist in administering the scheme.

Northern Territory—entitled to delegate its powers to one or more of the committee members or to a licensed managing agent (agent conduct is regulated under legislation).

Queensland—although the body corporate is prohibited from delegating its powers, it is authorised to appoint a body corporate manager to provide administrative services or exercise the authority of an executive member of the committee.

South Australia—the strata corporation is entitled to appoint a management committee to carry out most of its functions, duties and powers except where it requires a unanimous resolution. The committee is also unable to set the budget on behalf of the strata corporation or to raise a large amount of money through a special levy.

Delegation of the body corporate's powers, by region (cont'd)

The strata corporation may delegate the same powers, functions and duties to the strata manager.

Tasmania—may appoint a committee of management (by ordinary resolution) to act on their behalf. The committee may generally exercise any powers of the body corporate and may appoint a manager (by ordinary resolution) to carry out delegated powers and functions related to administration, management and control of the common property.

Victoria—the committee has all the powers and functions of the owners corporation and can delegate some powers to others to make day-to-day decisions without the need to call a general meeting. These powers may also be delegated to a professional manager.

Western Australia—may delegate its power to a 'council' (executive committee), which is governed by legislation and the scheme by-laws. The body corporate can further divide power by appointing a professional strata manager to perform its functions (although legal compliance still rests with each individual owner). Strata managers do not need to hold a licence or have any specific qualifications.

Source: Everton-Moore K, Ardill A, Guilding C, Warnken J 2006, 'The law of strata title in Australia: A jurisdictional stocktake', *Australia Property Law Journal*, 13.

Common property

For most owners of strata property, maintaining their private property is their biggest responsibility. Private property boundaries for each unit are usually formed by the interior face, the median or middle of the exterior face of walls, floors and ceilings, or—in the case of some single-storey properties—the exterior face of walls.

In most places in Australia, the following constitute common property:

☛ *External walls.* This includes doors and windows within those walls (although residents are usually responsible for keeping windows clean, even if they are common property).

☛ *The slab dividing two storeys.* Unless specifically stated on the strata plan, this is the dividing slab between two storeys of a unit or one storey from a useable rooftop area (such as a garden or courtyard).

☛ *Balcony doors and windows.* This can vary so it's wise to check your strata plan.

☛ *Floors and floorboards.* This includes ramps or stairways and any magnesite finish on a floor or tiling attached to the original floor.

☛ *Ceiling and cornices.* This can also vary so it's wise to check your strata plan.

☛ *Pipes* that service common areas or more than one unit.

☛ *Electrical wiring* that services common areas or more than one unit.

Figures 5.2 to 5.4 (overleaf) show some typical distinctions between common property and private property. Please note, these are *typical* distinctions and can vary depending on which state or territory you live in.

For state-by-state examples of what is considered common property, see appendix A.

Figure 5.2: typical common property boundaries — individual unit

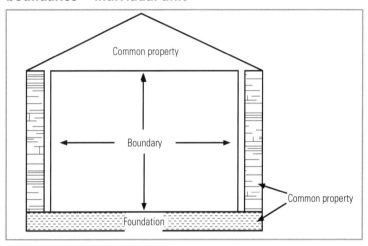

Figure 5.3: typical common property boundaries — strata plan

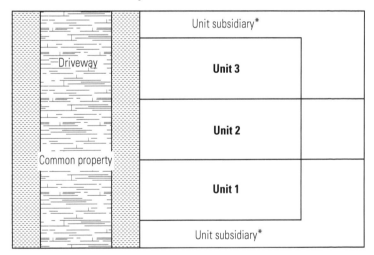

* A 'unit subsidiary' is an area for the exclusive use of a particular unit, for example, a carport or garden.

Figure 5.4: overhanging eaves

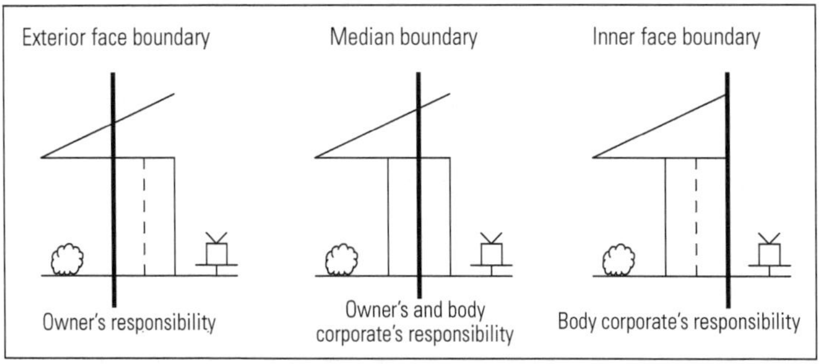

Exterior face boundary   Median boundary   Inner face boundary

Owner's responsibility   Owner's and body corporate's responsibility   Body corporate's responsibility

Responsibilities of owners

Just as bodies corporate have certain responsibilities to the unit owners in the strata scheme, owners and residents also must abide by certain rules and laws. These relate to by-laws/ rules introduced by the body corporate and to state-based laws contained in body corporate legislation.

By-laws/rules

As mentioned, all bodies corporate must abide by state-based by-laws/rules but may also create their own by-laws at general meetings. These laws apply to both owners and tenants and must be provided in writing within seven days of occupancy. These by-laws may be changed or abolished and new ones may be introduced by a body corporate by way of a special resolution (with the support of 75 per cent of unit owners).

By-laws/rules can differ in number and type from state to state, but generally apply to the following areas:

➥ *Appearance of units.* Owners and tenants must maintain the outside of their units in an acceptable manner. This includes not keeping anything outside their units that

101

is not in keeping with the overall appearance of the strata scheme.

- ↪ *Behaviour.* Owners and tenants should act appropriately when on common property, this includes dressing adequately and not using language or making gestures that may offend or embarrass other residents. Residents are also responsible for ensuring that anyone they invite onto the property behaves appropriately.

- ↪ *Noise.* Residents may not make excessive noise — either in their own units or on common property — that may disturb the peaceful enjoyment of other residents. This also applies to invited guests. Owners usually have to cover or treat their floor so as to minimise the noise that walking on them can cause for other residents below or next door (this doesn't apply to 'wet' areas).

- ↪ *Damaging common property.* Owners/tenants may not damage or otherwise alter any part of common property, including structures and landscaping, without the consent of the body corporate.

- ↪ *Obstructing common property.* Owners/tenants may not stop the lawful activity of other residents on common property. Also, it is usually required that residents advise the body corporate if they plan to move large items of furniture through common areas.

- ↪ *Littering common property.* Residents may not toss rubbish, dust, dirt or any other waste onto common property that may interfere with others' enjoyment of the common property.

- ↪ *General garbage disposal.* Residents must manage their waste appropriately, that is, store outside bins in a contained manner and keep them clean. They must put out their bins for collection in the designated area within

12 hours of collection and bring them in again within 12 hours after collection.

- *Clothes drying.* In most strata schemes, permission from the body corporate is required if residents wish to hang washing in view of other residents, such as over balconies or on clothes horses on front porches. Clothing hanging on common property clothes lines can only be there for a reasonable amount of time.

- *Vehicles.* Vehicles must park in designated areas. In special circumstances, permission can usually be sought from the body corporate to park on common property for a short period of time.

- *Children.* Bodies corporate may not use their by-laws to prohibit children living within the strata scheme. However, children are not usually permitted to play in internal common areas and in most strata schemes must be supervised when playing in external areas that may pose a danger to them, such as a laundry or where there are cars.

- *Pets.* Permission to keep an animal is usually required from bodies corporate. Most state legislation prohibits bodies corporate from refusing 'reasonable' requests in this area.

- *Storing dangerous goods.* Residents must usually get permission from a body corporate to store dangerous goods in their units, such as flammable liquids (unless being used for domestic purposes).

Occupational health and safety

Every body corporate is responsible for maintaining a safe environment for residents, guests, employees and any contractors who may work in common property areas within the site. State-based occupational health and safety (OH&S) Acts stipulate that the body corporate, as a site owner, will face penalties if a safe environment is not maintained (as far as is reasonably practical).

Active OH&S inspections should be conducted regularly. In Queensland the legislation stipulates every 12 months (at a minimum) and this has been wisely used as the minimum requirement across the national strata safety industry to meet the 'taking all reasonable actions' requirement to meet your obligations.

In each state there are different penalties for failing to comply with legislation. In New South Wales, for example, breaches can attract fines of up to $1.65 million for owners corporations and $165 000 and up to five years' jail for individuals. In Queensland it's fines of up to $750 000 for bodies corporate and $150 000 and three years' jail for individuals; in Victoria fines of up to $943 290 exist per offence for a company/owners corporation and $188 658 per offence for an individual with a jail sentence of five years.

Even worse, insurance won't usually cover the fines. Fines and penalties are in almost every case not covered by any insurance policy. A fine shows you have not fulfilled your obligations under law and this is specifically excluded from insurance cover. An insurance company cannot go to jail for you either.

Ignorance is no excuse. Non-action tends to be viewed by courts as a form of negligence leading to increased penalties. The OH&S regime and legislation has been in force for more than 20 years and has received massive amounts of media publicity. Courts are now fining those who admit they did nothing to meet their OH&S obligations lower amounts than those who claim ignorance or fabricate a defence at the last moment. They are calling it a 'utilitarian plea' that saves wasting court time.

As part of building regulations, most states have a formal process in place for assessing and maintaining occupational health and safety and 'essential safety measures' (those items that ensure adequate levels of fire safety and protection for people in the building and their escape from the building in case of a fire). While there are minor variations between states, the *Building Code of Australia (BCA)* established in July 1997, controls the process for auditing properties for compliance. Enforcing the code in each state is the responsibility of the Municipal Building Surveyor, Building Certifier and the Chief Officer, or Authorised Fire Officer (fire authority).

For more information, search the internet for your state- or territory-based legislation:

- Australian Capital Territory — *BCA 1996–97*

- New South Wales — *Statutory Fire Safety Measures*

- Northern Territory — *BCA 1996–97*

- Queensland — *Fire Safety Act Part 9A, Building Fire Safety Regulations (1991)*

- South Australia — *South Australian Regulation 76 of Development Regulations, Minister's Specification SA76*

- Tasmania — *The Building Act (2000)*

- Victoria — *Building Regulations (2006)*

- Western Australia — *BCA 1996–97.*

Contractor safety

It's vitally important that the body corporate makes sure any contractors that come on site — such as plumbers, electricians and carpenters — are qualified, insured and operate in a safe manner. The consequences of not ensuring this can be devastating, as demonstrated in the following case study.

Case study: contractor insurance

The body corporate overseeing the *Schofield Towers* low-rise apartment block engaged the services of Sparkle Cleaning Services to do a thorough clean of the building's hallways, stairs and foyer area.

Soon after they had finished the job and left the premises, 81-year-old Marj Stockdale was walking through the foyer area on a walking stick when she slipped on a puddle of water left behind by the cleaners. Marj was badly injured, breaking a hip and ending up in hospital.

Marj's family decide to sue. Their first target was the cleaning company; but, discovering that Sparkle don't have insurance or the means to cover the claim, they decide to go after the body corporate. Although the body corporate had its own insurance, when it got to court, their insurance company argued that the body corporate should contribute personally to the claim as they had contributed to the situation by being negligent and engaging an uninsured contractor. This line of argument is successful and the body corporate is left to foot the bill for Mrs Stockdale's medical bills and legal fees plus additional compensation.

To make matters worse, the nature of the injury and resulting legal issue meant that a WorkCover investigation was initiated and the body corporate was left facing fines of up to $1 million pending the outcome of the investigation.

This case study reinforces the importance of understanding what your insurance policy is covering and of seeking expert advice from insurers.

What to check

To avoid getting caught out by unqualified or ill-insured contractors, the body corporate should check the following when engaging a contractor:

- *ABN*. Make sure the contractor has an Australian Business Number and check whether the structure is a company, partnership, sole trader or trust (this will impact on their maximum level of financial liability).

- *Licences/registrations*. Most contractors should hold some kind of state-based industry licence or registration although this will depend on the state and the industry.

- *Insurance*. Depending on the type of tradesperson or other professional you are contracting out services to, they might hold either public liability, professional indemnity, product liability or workers compensation insurance, or a combination of these. Insurance is a national issue and does not vary much by state. There is usually no legislated minimum requirement for insurance; however, $5 million is often used as a minimum for public liability in the body corporate sector.

What next?

One aspect of strata life that buyers often overlook is the numerous fees associated with being a part of a body corporate. Chapter 6 looks at these in more detail.

Chapter 6

Fees and financial management

As discussed in chapter 5, one of the main responsibilities of the body corporate is raising and managing fees and keeping track of its finances. Bodies corporate collect fees from unit owners and unit owners have unlimited financial liability to the body corporate. This means that you may face unforeseen (and unfavourable!) financial consequences because of poor financial management on the part of the body corporate.

Case study: striking unexpected fees after purchase

Having recently got engaged to be married, Emalie and Brad looked anxiously around for a unit to buy near Emalie's father. They thought they'd struck gold when they found the perfect place at just the right price.

In their excitement, they signed the contract of sale and hastily bought the unit. Both had never lived out of home before and

---

Case study: striking unexpected fees after purchase *(cont'd)*

didn't fully understand what a body corporate is and what their rights and obligations were. They also neglected to undertake due diligence to conduct research on that particular body corporate prior to purchase.

Three months after Emalie and Brad moved into their unit, a special resolution was passed by 75 per cent of members of the body corporate to undertake underpinning work at a cost of $75000. Unfortunately, the couple did not review the minutes of the last general meeting of the body corporate before the purchase so had no idea this work was even being talked about.

Had Emalie and Brad reviewed the minutes they would have seen that underpinning work was required and proposed although not yet confirmed at the time. Furthermore, the minutes would have revealed that the body corporate planned to fund this work by having a special levy.

It was decided that each of the five members of the body corporate would pay a special levy of $15000 to fund the underpinning work. As a member of the body corporate, Emalie and Brad must now immediately pay $15000 in addition to their purchase price and their ordinary obligations to the body corporate.

This doesn't mean that Emalie and Brad bought a bad unit. However, had they known the situation, they probably would have paid a different price for it. The existence of a sinking fund or an imminent special levy is neither good nor bad in itself, but knowledge of it enables you to make better informed decisions.

It is generally the body corporate's role to:

- set fees to cover expenses such as general administration, maintenance and insurance

- raise one-off special fees for extraordinary expenses
- pay insurance premiums
- pay contractors and other suppliers
- pay wages to employees and managers (if applicable)
- invest money and maintain a bank account
- recover money owed and charge interest as a penalty
- borrow money
- keep financial records, including preparing annual financial statements.

A body corporate may keep its financial records in paper form or in an electronic software program such as MYOB. How well the accounts are kept often depends on the level of complexity of the body corporate's financial affairs and the level of skill of the record keeper. To meet its obligations to the Australian Taxation Office (ATO), bodies corporate should keep:

- income records (including tax invoices, receipts, credit card statements and bank statements)
- expenditure records (including purchase invoices, purchase receipts containing an ABN, cheque butts, credit card statements and bank statements)
- assets and liabilities records (including an assets register, depreciation schedules, tax returns, unpaid invoices and lists of creditors and debtors).

For more information on these requirements, refer to the ATO website at <www.ato.gov.au>.

Fees

Strata fees are usually paid quarterly, half-yearly or yearly, depending on the arrangement set down by the body corporate.

Most bodies corporate tend to opt for quarterly which seems to be workable for owners and the body corporate but the financial period can be anything to which people agree.

Unit entitlement and liability

Each unit in a strata scheme pays fees based on their 'unit entitlement' (called lot entitlement in some states) or 'unit liability' (called lot liability in some states). When a unit is sold it has a specified number of entitlement and liability units attached to it. Unit liability is the proportion of the body corporate expenses that a particular unit owner must pay. It is, in effect, the proportion of the total body corporate expenses that you as an owner are responsible for.

Unit entitlement reflects the unit owner's share of ownership in the assets, in other words, the common property. It also reflects a fair sharing of the body corporate's expenses (excluding Victoria) and dictates the entitlement of a unit owner if the body corporate is dissolved (for example, if the entire building is sold, destroyed or demolished) and voting rights at body corporate meetings.

In most states, unit entitlement and liability will be combined under one heading of unit entitlement/lot entitlement. In Victoria, for example, unit entitlement should usually represent the value of the units as a proportion of the total value of all units. By contrast, unit liability should be based on a fair sharing of expenses of the body corporate. Table 6.1 shows which states and territories have just unit liability or entitlement, or both.

Table 6.1: unit/lot entitlement and liability, by region

Region	Unit/lot entitlement	Unit/lot liability
ACT	✓	✗
NSW	✓	✗

Region	Unit/lot entitlement	Unit/lot liability
NT	✓	✗
Qld*	✓	✗
SA	✓	✗
Tas.*	✓	✗
Vic.	✓	✓
WA	✓	✗

*There are currently two variations on unit entitlement in Queensland and Tasmania. There is a general unit of entitlement and there may also be a special unit entitlement in Tasmania.

Basic strata fees

Basic strata fees (sometimes called administration fees or levies) will vary according to the size of the strata property and the complexity of managing and maintaining the common property. Having a look at the amenities and imagining how much they would cost to maintain will give you some idea of how high the fees might be for a property you're interested in buying. For example, if the scheme has a pool, tennis court, gym, lifts and a 24-hour concierge, you can guess that the fees will be much higher than in a unit that has none of these facilities. Ocean views can be beautiful (and probably one of the main reasons you bought the property in the first place), but salty breezes have a habit of eroding paintwork, rusting metalwork (including wire-strung fences) and increasing concrete 'cancer' (that is, concrete spalling). Fixing such damage requires funding from sinking fund savings, special levies or borrowing.

Figures 6.1 to 6.4 show how fees are typically broken down for a variety of unit types. These figures are all taken from actual unit blocks.

Figure 6.1: fees for a simple six-unit block

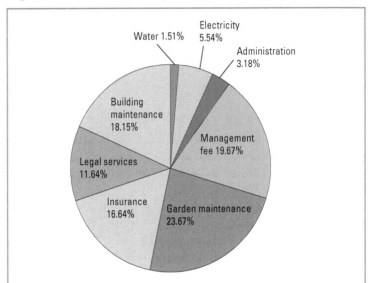

Figure 6.2: fees for a 27-unit block (units are all double-storey)

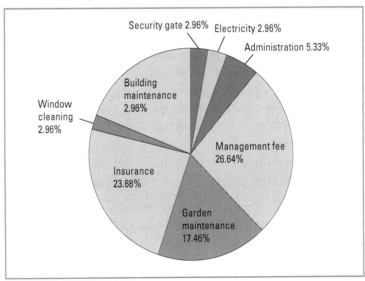

Figure 6.3: fees for a 54-unit complex

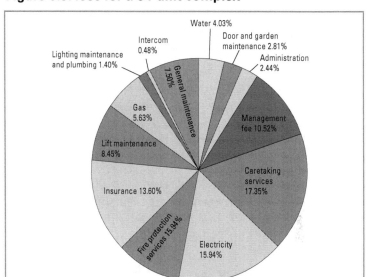

Figure 6.4: fees for a 150-unit complex

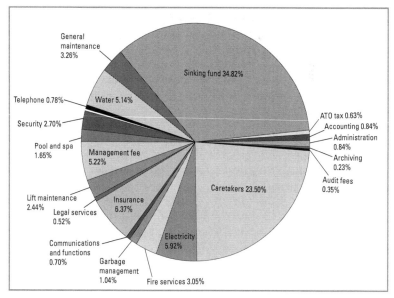

Many people get upset about these fees but it's hard to understand why. Although these fees are specific to bodies corporate, if you own a house you will have to pay for maintenance and all other 'operational' expenses yourself so there is no real difference. Actually, in a body corporate, it's likely that the many maintenance costs are cheaper for the individual owner—the electricity bill may be larger, but it's shared. The only difference between body corporate fees and house maintenance costs is that if you have a house you will have a little more control over the timing of the expense.

Body corporate fees (also called levies) are a mandatory part of strata living. Unit owners must pay their annual and special fees according to their unit liability or unit entitlements. If fees are not paid, unit owners lose the right to vote on all matters that require an ordinary resolution. They can still attend meetings and vote on matters that require a special or unanimous resolution (see table 6.2 for a state-by-state breakdown). The body corporate can charge interest on delayed fees and can take legal action to recover outstanding money.

Fees must be determined at each AGM, and decided by a majority vote. All unit owners should then be advised in writing of what they have to pay and by when.

With all the body corporate is responsible for, it must obviously bring in enough money to pay for its activities. Owners (and bodies corporate) usually have to make decisions about two kinds of funding: how to best provide for operational or administrative costs (such as paying for cleaning or gardening); and how best to fund future 'major anticipated capital expenditure'.

Most often (there are always exceptions), operational and administrative are best covered by regular contributions—monthly or quarterly levies. (You might be surprised to know how many bodies corporate access funding for their insurance premiums, usually considered an operational item.)

When it comes to funding current or future major capital expenditure, there are three forms of funding: saving by having regular levies to a sinking fund; raising one-off special levies; and borrowing. The body corporate and its owners should consider each of these options (or a mix of options) on its merits and make their decision according to their particular situation.

Table 6.2: the rights of owners who fail to pay their fees, by region

Region	Rights
ACT	Voting rights for ordinary and special resolutions are not extended to unit owners in arrears. However this does not apply to motions requiring unanimous resolutions and to owners corporations that comprise three or fewer units.
NSW	Voting rights are not given to unit owners who have not paid their contributions (unless the vote requires a unanimous resolution).
NT	Unit holders in arrears do not have voting rights, unless a unanimous resolution is required.
Qld	If the unit owner has fees outstanding at the time of the meeting, they may vote only on a resolution without dissent and may not participate in electing committee members.
SA	Unit holders in arrears do not have voting rights, unless a unanimous resolution is required.
Tas.	Nothing in the legislation prohibits owners from attending a meeting or voting.
Vic.	A unit owner whose fees are in arrears is not entitled to vote at a meeting, by poll, or by ballot unless a special resolution or unanimous resolution is required.
WA	Lot owners in arrears are not able to vote at meetings (unless it is a resolution requiring a unanimous resolution or a resolution without dissent).

Administrative and operational expenses

This fund covers all recurring day-to-day or operational expenses of the body corporate including:

- the cost of maintaining common property, for example, garden maintenance and utility bills
- paying insurance premiums
- any other recurrent funds not covered by either the sinking fund or a special levy.

The owners should consider a budget at least annually and determine how they will fund these expenses. Usually a regular administration fee is the choice though bodies corporate, like many businesses, often choose to obtain 'premium funding' to pay for their insurance. In theory, they could have a special levy or borrow, but that's usually considered to be less convenient for operational expenses.

Major capital expenditure

When it comes to funding major capital expenditure, owners and bodies corporate have three options: to save in a sinking fund; to have a special levy; or to borrow. They could also have a mix of these funding methods. Each of these means of funding has its advantages and disadvantages and so each situation needs to be considered on its merits.

Anticipated major capital expenditure (or long-term capital maintenance) might include:

- buying shared equipment, such as mowers or washing machines
- painting common areas
- replacing fixtures or fittings in common areas, such a light fittings, blinds or doors

- modernising or replacing the lift or the air-conditioning
- replacing the roof
- refurbishing the building
- replacing windows and balconies (usually, but not always, these items are common property).

The three forms of strata funding are discussed further in chapter 8.

Unbudgeted items

Occasionally a cost will come up that the body corporate didn't budget for, usually because it has come about through a special request to buy or upgrade a one-off item for the property. This might be the result of a decision to install a security system, a spa to accompany an existing pool, replace a perimeter fence, or purchase more equipment for the communal gym. Or you may have to deal with a legal requirement imposed on the body corporate such as a council fire order.

Again, the body corporate has three options to fund it: using the savings in a sinking fund; raising a special levy; or borrowing (discussed later).

What next?

Much of the work of a body corporate is achieved through the elected executive committee. How these committees are elected, what they do and how they conduct meetings is covered in the next chapter.

Chapter 7

Executive committees and meetings

One of the big differences between living in a 'good' body corporate and a 'bad' one is the character of the people imposing the by-laws and making the decisions about what you can and can't do on your own property.

The executive committee of a body corporate is the group of elected owners (or their representatives) who are responsible for running and maintaining the block of units, apartment building, strip of shops, office building or whatever the structure of the body corporate is. The maximum allowable number of committee members varies from state to state as indicated in table 7.1.

Table 7.1: numbers of committee members, by region (according to regional legislation)

Region	What is the minimum number of the committee?	What is the maximum number (not including the manager)?
ACT	3 people	7 people
NSW	1 person	9 people

Table 7.1 *(cont'd)*: numbers of committee members, by region (according to regional legislation)

Region	What is the minimum number of the committee?	What is the maximum number (not including the manager)?
NT	2 people	7 people
Qld	1 person	7 people
SA	No minimum	No maximum
Tas.	3 people	No maximum
Vic.	3 people	12 people
WA	3 people	7 people

No matter what number your state allows, it's critical to make a good decision about what the maximum number of committee members should be in your situation. With the increasing importance of corporate governance in our companies, there is a lot of research and evidence on the 'optimum' number of people in a group to make decisions. I believe we should apply this company research and experience to bodies corporate.

Contrary to many people's belief, more is not necessarily better. Some people think that the larger the body corporate the larger the committee it should have. This is not the case in my experience. The committee is not a parliament elected to represent owners. It shouldn't work on the principle of one committee member for so many owners.

A committee is a small working group; its job is to get things done on behalf of owners and its authority is delegated to it by all owners in a general meeting. Therefore, the size should be determined by the social dynamics of how people work together. In my experience, three to five is a good working number. You shouldn't place undue attention on the possibility that members might not be able to attend meetings so that a larger committee might be required. If members can't attend, they shouldn't be on the committee.

The original owner of a strata scheme has certain obligations and responsibilities, the most significant of these being to convene and hold the first annual general meeting (AGM). In New South Wales, this must occur within two months of establishing the body corporate, irrespective of whether or not the original owner still owns any units in the scheme. In Victoria, it may happen any time within six months of registration with Land Victoria. In the Northern Territory, the corporation's powers are restricted during the 'initial period', which ends when more than one-third of the units have been sold to parties not including the developer.

If the original owner still owns at least 50 per cent or more of the scheme and a vote by special resolution or poll is requested, the value of the original owner's vote is reduced to one-third of his unit entitlement.

Queensland is the only state that stipulates in legislation that the meetings must be held within 15 kilometres of the strata scheme. In South Australia the location must be 'reasonably convenient' for the majority of members.

The first AGM

The first body corporate AGM must be held within a given time frame from when the body corporate plan is registered. This is stipulated in each state or territory's legislation (see table 7.2, overleaf).

Although this varies slightly between states, at the first AGM the original owner must usually give the body corporate:

- all plans, specifications, certificates (other than certificates of title for units), diagrams and other documents (including policies of insurance) that relate to the site

Table 7.2: meeting notice requirements, by region

Region	Time frame for AGM from registration	Time frame for notice of the AGM	Notice of motions required	Must motions be included in the meeting notice?	Maximum time frame to conduct AGM after end of year
ACT	6 months	14 days unless a unanimous resolution is required, then 21 days	14 days unless a unanimous resolution is required, then 21 days	Yes	Within 15 months of preceding AGM
NSW	Within 2 months of one-third of all units being sold	7 days	7 days (in writing)	Yes	30 days either side of the first AGM anniversary
NT	3 months	14 days unless a unanimous resolution is required, then 21 days	14 days unless a unanimous resolution is required, then 21 days	No	Within 15 months of preceding AGM

Region	Time frame for AGM from registration	Time frame for notice of the AGM	Notice of motions required	Must motions be included in the meeting notice?	Maximum time frame to conduct AGM after end of year
Qld	Within 2 months of the original owner having sold more than half of the units or when the scheme has been established for 6 months	7 days	Prior to the end of the year	Yes	2 months of the first AGM anniversary. 3 months from end of financial year
SA	12 months	14 days	14 days	No	3 months
Tas.	Within 3 months or after half of the units have been sold (whichever comes first)	7 days	None specified. Proposed unanimous resolutions must be included in notice	No	Within 15 months of preceeding AGM
Vic.	6 months	14 days	14 days	Yes	90 days
WA	3 months	No specific time	14 days	No	N/A

Source: Adapted from NCTI. Additional tables and information are available from the National Community Titles Institute website. Visit <www.ncti.org.au>.

- the certificate of title for the common property, the strata roll (the list of all owners in the body corporate) and any notices or other records relating to the strata scheme (in Victoria a duplicate certificate of title is not issued)

- the body corporate's common seal (the rubber stamp used to authorise documents; all bodies corporate must have one — see table 7.3)

- any contracts, leases and licences binding or benefiting the body corporate

- copies of any warranties or guarantees (including the names of the companies, tradespeople or suppliers who provided them)

- a copy of the relevant legislation pertaining to the state or territory

- the accounting records and most recent financial statements.

Table 7.3: common seal reqirements, by region

Region	What must it be used for?	Who can witnesses the affixing of the seal?	Who can the use of the seal be delegated to?
ACT	Documents authorised by the resolution of the body corporate	2 members unless if only one owner	Not able to be delegated
NSW	All documents required to be served by the owners corporation	2 committee members, owners or the managing agent	To the strata manager

Region	What must it be used for?	Who can witnesses the affixing of the seal?	Who can the use of the seal be delegated to?
NT	On documents approved by the secretary or by resolution	2 or more committee members or owners or the secretary and another committee member	To executive committee member
Qld	Any instrument authorised by the body corporate	2 committee members or manager	To the managing agent
SA	Only in the manner directed by the corporation at the meeting	Any two of the: presiding officer, treasurer or secretary	To a member or employee of the corporation
Tas.	Only by resolution of body corporate or committee of management	2 members unless if only one owner	To the manager
Vic.	On documents specified as requiring the seal	2 unit owners who own separate units and who are members	To committee, manager, unit owner, chairperson, secretary and employee
WA	Only by authority of the strata council	2 members of the council or an ordinary member if only 1 owner	Members (as with all strata council powers)

Source: Adapted from NCTI. Additional tables and information are available from the National Community Titles Institute website. Visit <www.ncti.org.au>.

All owners listed on the strata roll must be invited to attend the first AGM. During this meeting, a number of motions must be decided, including:

- insurance cover
- determining by-laws/rules
- fees
- electing the executive committee
- restricted matters (any matters that need a special or unanimous resolution or which the body corporate has decided must go to a general meeting such as major capital works or the selling off of common property)
- appointment of an auditor, caretaker and/or body corporate manager (if necessary).

Who sits on an executive committee?

As mentioned, the best size for a committee is unlikely to be the maximum allowed in your state; it's better to have a good working group of three to five. You might have a slightly larger group if you know that there will be a changeover in the future and you want to introduce a few people to bring them up to speed with how things are run.

Office holders are usually elected at the committee meeting following the first AGM. Even if there is a strata managing agent and certain duties have been delegated to them, the secretary and treasurer are still able to exercise their powers if they choose to do so. In most instances the strata managing agent performs all the functions of the secretary and treasurer and they operate in a supervisory position.

In a scheme where there are only two units, the committee comprises the two owners. Every executive committee must have (as a minimum) a chairperson and a secretary, so in the case of a two-unit body corporate, each person could assume one of these roles or one person could conduct both roles. Any decision made by the committee is usually treated as a decision by the body corporate provided the motion does not relate to a restricted matter that must be decided by the body corporate at a general meeting.

In addition to the members, each committee will vote in a chairperson, secretary and a treasurer, all of whom have specific functions. These include:

- *Chairperson:* The role of the chairperson is to conduct meetings and to decide on issues relating to voting and procedure. When electing a chair, you want someone who can hold their own — someone who is firm but fair. Experience on a board (or at least with chairing meetings) is important. This person will also be representing the whole committee in any disputes, to local council, and with suppliers/contractors. They should therefore be articulate and credible and be an overall good 'face' of the committee. Often it's a good idea for an external person to chair a meeting so the chair of the body corporate and chair of a meeting may be different.

- *Secretary:* The secretary will be responsible for: organising meetings (of the committee and any other meeting that might be required, such as with the local council or a legal representative); preparing and distributing minutes of meetings; attending to correspondence on behalf of the body corporate; and maintaining administrative and secretarial records of the body corporate (including strata roll).

  An ideal secretary will have experience in writing correspondence and taking minutes, be organised and efficient. Nowadays, someone who is handy with a computer and is familiar with email is also essential.

Many of these tasks could also be undertaken by a body corporate manager (discussed in chapter 5).

☛ *Treasurer:* Treasurers issue levy notices, receipt and bank money on behalf of the body corporate, prepare financial statements and other financial records and maintain accounting records. This role can be relatively straightforward if the body corporate is small (under 10 units), or complex and time-consuming if we're talking about a 400-unit apartment building or 100-outlet shopping mall. If the body corporate is a large one, you will really need someone who can confidently navigate a spreadsheet, balance a profit and loss statement and has a good grasp of accounting principles. Attention to detail is a must.

The regulations regarding whether or not a manager can chair a meeting varies across Australia, as shown in table 7.4.

Table 7.4: who can chair a meeting?

Region	Can the manager chair a meeting?
ACT	✓
NSW	✓
NT	✓
Qld	✓
SA	✗
Tas.	✓
Vic.	✓
WA	✓

Off the plan

If you're buying off the plan, it's critical that you attend the body corporate's first AGM. This is usually held when one-third of the strata properties within it have been sold (the time period within which the first AGM is to be held varies with state or territory legislation). At this point, the developer will still have control over the building or units as the owner of the majority of the units.

The first meeting is when the body corporate vote whether to accept the by-laws/rules laid down by the developer's lawyers. It's important that you have your say because the by-laws/rules will affect most of what you will and will not be able to do to your property.

Feeling vulnerable is understandable at a first meeting. There may be a lot going on, some owners may have already formed relationships and you may feel like an outsider. They may be discussing issues that go right over your head. Even so, don't allow yourself to be bombarded by the developer. If you don't understand something, ask for it to be explained more clearly. They've probably done this numerous times before.

In times gone by, the majority of units being developer-owned at this point has meant that the developer's voting power has far outweighed that of other owners. Laws in most states have now been amended to limit the voting powers of developers. Some developers may hold proxies for other units if they have the owners signed up to their own finance packages. A few examples are:

- *New South Wales* — there are restrictions on what can be done during the 'initial period'. The initial period is the period from when the owners corporation is registered until one-third of the unit entitlements are transferred from the original owner/developer.

  There are restrictions on the owners corporation borrowing money, altering the common property, making certain by-laws and entering into contractual arrangements.

Proxy votes and powers of attorney will not be accepted where the proxy or power of attorney is given to the original owner by the unit owner under the contract of sale for the purchase of that owner's unit.

- *Victoria* — a developer or any other person cannot request, either verbally or in a contract, a proxy or power of attorney from a new owner, or any owner. This action would result in a fine. The owners corporation must act in good faith, which applies even when the owners corporation is controlled by the original owner/developer.

- *Queensland* — the original owner/developer must act in the best interests of the body corporate. No prohibition on proxies.

- *Western Australia* — proxies cannot be used by any person who has an interest in an agreement entered into with the strata company unless they meet certain criteria as specified in section 50A of the *Strata Titles Act*.

Case study: attending the first AGM

Siobhan, a private school teacher, purchased a strata unit within a new golf course development off the plan. She was motivated by the opportunity to pay only a five per cent deposit and by the considered stamp duty savings she could make because construction had not yet begun. Construction would take at least two years so she had ample time to arrange her finances.

Some months later Siobhan received notice of the body corporate's first AGM. The notice said that a committee would be elected, fees would be fixed and the proposed annual budget considered. Siobhan had already planned a ski trip with friends on the day of the AGM so she asked her boyfriend, Stefan, to attend the meeting as her proxy.

Stefan went along but was overwhelmed by the volume of information presented. When the time came to vote Stefan stuck with the majority so as not to make himself conspicuous and on the reckoning that the majority must be right.

On settlement, Siobhan was disappointed at how small her unit was. Her courtyard looked nothing like those in the promotional material and the colour scheme was not what she expected. Worse still, there were large gaps in the cornices and 'water hammer' occurred whenever she turned on the tap.

A few weeks later Siobhan received an invoice requiring her to pay various fees to the body corporate including a charge for garden maintenance in the central courtyard. Alarm bells began to ring.

Siobhan inspected the body corporate's records and found that a quorum was not present at the AGM. She hoped this meant that the decisions were not binding but was dismayed when her solicitor told her that the meeting could proceed without a quorum and that the resolutions were interim for 28 days and confirmed on the 29th day unless challenged by owners. That time had passed and Siobhan lamented not reading more closely the meeting minutes she'd received by post.

The records also revealed that a garden contractor had been appointed for 20 years. His rates appeared excessive. Siobhan called the developer and was advised that the resolution was binding — a contract had been entered into and there was nothing she could do about it. During the conversation Siobhan mentioned the gaps above the cornice and the water hammer issues and was told that this is usual and acceptable in new properties.

Increasingly worried, Siobhan again contacted her solicitor, this time about the garden contractor. He confirmed that the resolutions

Case study: attending the first AGM *(cont'd)*

had become binding because of the time lag and advised Siobhan that she may have a case if the amount payable to the contractor does not reflect a reasonable market rate, as the developer has a duty of good faith to act in the body corporate's best interests. She was advised to get some quotes from other contractors as a comparison and told of the option to apply to court to have the contract set aside.

Siobhan is currently speaking to other unit owners in her strata scheme to ascertain if they are interested in pursuing court action.

In relation to the building defects, Siobhan was told that she might have avoided or delayed settlement had she engaged an expert to inspect the property beforehand. No warranty insurance is available because the builder is still trading. Again she appears to have valid grounds to issue legal proceedings—this time against the builder—but will be required to finance the action herself.

Setting up a new executive committee

When setting up a new committee, you have the opportunity to bring in a mix of people who can serve the body corporate well. It's best to have an odd number of members for voting reasons—that way the chair can't exercise a casting vote. Although, this can sometimes be a good thing in a small committee where the chair has a moral right to vote for their views.

Choose carefully. Sometimes the people who self-nominate are the ones you don't want on your committee because they either want to stir things up or like the idea of wielding power over the other owners. Ask nominators to explain what contribution they could make, and what ideas for changes or work they will propose for the body corporate. Ask if they are investors or if they plan to live in the unit. Ask how long they plan to stay. Investors and short-term owners are not likely to want to fix longer term problems, but will rather look at stop-gaps to defer the need to spend money. They probably won't be interested in contributing to the sinking fund for the same reason.

Beware of voting developer representatives onto the committee. These people are likely to hold up any action the body corporate may want to take against the developer for sloppy workmanship. Ask anyone who nominates to declare if they are affiliated with the developer in any way (including professionally, financially or personally).

Mix it up

An effective executive committee will have representation from a good mix of people. That means, a good mix of experience — both life and work — and views about how things should be managed. If you live in a high-rise apartment block, it's a good idea to have people from a variety of levels (top floor, bottom floors and a mix of in between) so there can be no suggestion that 'the top floor people don't understand how the trees are blocking the views of the lower floor people' and the like. An ideal committee consists not of similar people who share similar views, but of people who are open to fair and frank discussions about issues and who can talk their way to a decision.

It's great to have someone who knows something about money management and running budgets — an accountant if possible. Some larger bodies corporate can be managing budgets in the millions, so you want someone who can handle that amount of accounting activity.

Someone who knows something about building and construction is also an advantage. Much of the work of bodies corporate is managing building maintenance and repairs and having someone who has an advanced knowledge of building maintenance (like a professional builder) will be invaluable.

An owner with legal experience is another person you want on your committee. Paying for legal advice if a dispute arises can take a large chunk out of your budget so not having to pay for this will benefit everyone. Even having someone who knows how to use legal jargon to write a scary letter to a noisy neighbour or dodgy contractor (preferably on legal firm letterhead) goes a long way to nipping potential legal issues in the bud.

Of course, smaller bodies corporate won't have such a big pool of unit owners to draw from. In this case, it's best to chose people who plan to live there for an extended period and who seem to have a genuine interest in doing what's best for all owners and residents, not just themselves.

Remember: when the executive committee is elected, this group will decide policy for the property and, in effect, run it. And just because you don't know anyone else in the room, it doesn't mean no-one else does — they may form a mini power group of mates.

Case study: a flawed body corporate

The body corporate at 185 Winchester Street employed a contractor to undertake extensive painting, plastering and tiling work in the apartment building's foyer. The contractor's quote simply contained the site address and a lump sum figure. No description of the work was set out.

Months later, the job was still not complete, partly because the contractor would work at other sites and only devote one or two days a week to Winchester Street. Nonetheless, he would submit weekly invoices expecting prompt payment.

Unhappy with the lack of progress, the body corporate soon stopped paying the invoices. The contractor's response was to write to the manager advising that he was suspending the work and planned to sue the body corporate for his outstanding invoices.

The body corporate decided to employ a consultant for advice on how to proceed. The consultant was unable to say how far the work had progressed because the contractor's quote was so short on detail about what the job entailed. He estimated, however, that perhaps 40 per cent of all necessary work had been undertaken. The body corporate had already paid 80 per cent of the contract price. Not surprisingly, the contractor was not motivated to return to the site and complete the work.

The body corporate then asked their legal representative about claiming on the builder's warranty insurance and was told that they might only have recourse to warranty insurance if the contractor were dead, disappeared or insolvent. Nevertheless, the lawyer requested a copy of the insurance certificate. The body corporate was unable to produce it.

The body corporate manager proceeded to obtain quotes from alternative contractors so the work could be finished. Of the four tradespeople contacted only one was willing to accept the job and his fee well exceeded the handyman's original quote.

Still hoping to minimise their losses, the body corporate asked their lawyer about its rights to sue the handyman for inconvenience, upset and costs. This action, they were told, would result in stagnation of the work until the matter was heard and determined by the state's civil tribunal.

The tasks for a new executive committee

Apart from choosing members, there is an enormous amount of work associated with setting up a new committee, particularly in bodies corporate that involve a number of units. Among the issues you need to deal with are:

- appointing a building manager

- appointing a strata/body corporate manager if not already appointed

- reviewing and creating by-laws/rules (and deciding how to enforce them)

- appointing subcommittees (if required)

- establishing maintenance contracts, including building maintenance, grounds maintenance and cleaning contracts.

Two last pieces of advice here:

- *Don't give your chair too much power.* You want all critical decision-making rights to rest evenly among the members.

- *Don't agree to any long-term contracts relating to the building.* Shorter term contracts will give you enough time to assess the contractor's performance.

Meeting lingo

Official meetings tend to have their own terms that may be foreign to you if you're not used to attending them. Some of these are:

- Minutes—the official, written record of the proceedings of a meeting.

- Motion — a proposal that is formally put forward at a meeting for the purpose of reaching a decision.

- Proxy — person appointed to represent another person at a meeting or meetings. The proxy is authorised to vote on behalf of the person they represent.

- Quorum — the number of members required to be present at a meeting to make decisions binding. If the block consists of only two units, the quorum is both members. In an executive committee, it is usually half of the elected committee members.

- Resolutions — decisions made, and documented, by ballot or at a meeting.

Influencing an established committee

In most cases, strata property buyers will be buying into an existing body corporate with an established committee. Looking around the properties within the body corporate and taking note of outside maintenance should give you a pretty good sense of how proactive the committee is. If the property is generally run down and looks unloved, the chances are you're buying into a body corporate that doesn't want to spend any money and has no interest in the aesthetics of the units within it. Reading the minutes of past meetings will give you an even better feel for how the existing committee approaches issues (see chapter 2 about obtaining minutes in your state or territory). How often are they meeting? Have they kept good minutes? Are members raising issues that are quickly dismissed? What work have they approved in the past three or four years and what has been denied? This is all very important information if you have grand plans for renovating your unit. Committees that block member requests may serve as warning signs that you may not be able to do everything you want. Inactive committees might not care what you do and proactive committees might dictate exactly *how* you do it. Of course this is generalising, but it doesn't hurt to prepare yourself.

Getting what you want

Some of the older, well-established executive committees may comprise elderly people who have lived in their units for a long time and are happy not to make any significant changes. They get the lawns mowed once a fortnight in spring and tend to look after their own gardens. That's fine, but they also probably have little disposable income to contribute to the body corporate. On the other hand, some of these older committees might have amassed quite a healthy reserve of money that they are loath to spend on aesthetic changes just in case of an unforeseen emergency that never seems to happen.

There are two ways to deal with committees that don't want to do anything: general persuasion and turning up the heat. General persuasion, if it's possible, is always going to be the better approach because it means you will (hopefully) preserve the relationship with your neighbours in the process of getting what you want. Start with all the logical arguments: *doing this work will increase the value of all our properties; a better presented block will attract better quality buyers and tenants which will benefit everyone; installing a security camera or a remote-controlled gate at the street entrance will enhance everyone's security.* For those older owners who plan to see out their days in their unit, appeal to their sense of family and the legacy they will leave: *don't you want to hand down a unit you are proud of and that has real value to your children?*

If calm influence doesn't do the trick, you may have to bring out the big guns. Lobby individual members of the executive committee with your proposal; invite them over for a cuppa and talk them through your plans, explaining why it will benefit everyone. If you live in a larger block of units, do a bulk letterbox drop of all owners, explaining your ideas and asking for their support. They can then sign a petition, come along to the next committee meeting and voice their support, or write a letter to the chairperson outlining their views.

If lack of funds is an issue, you can always propose that a special, one-off levy is introduced to cover the work. This will need to be tabled at the AGM or, if you feel it can't wait, an extraordinary general meeting (EGM/SGM) can be convened to discuss the issue. In order to call an EGM/SGM, you will either need a majority vote from the committee or, depending on which state or territory you are in, the signatures of at least a quarter of all unit owners.

Requesting that all owners put in additional money to fund a special project can be a tough ask and difficult to get through. That's where — if you're passionate enough about the project — you will need to do a lot of advance work rallying the support of your fellow owners and committee members, developing solid arguments for your proposal (preferably with evidence) and facing up to the meeting prepared for a heated debate on your proposal's merits. The following case study might give you food for thought.

Case study: influencing the body corporate

As a single mother with two girls aged under 10 living in a block of 24 flats, Rosie was concerned about the lack of security. In the previous two years there had been three break-ins in the block, one of which occurred while the residents were at home sleeping. In the block of units adjacent to them, a school-aged girl had gone missing from her home, and two streets away an elderly homeowner was bashed by an intruder, robbed and left for dead.

Case study: influencing the body corporate *(cont'd)*

Understandably, Rosie was concerned for her own safety, the safety of her girls and the safety of the other residents in her block.

The Gardenview Apartments where they lived were built in the early 1950s. The main lobby was easily accessible from the street through a common door that was left unlocked during the day. It was usually locked after dark, that is, if someone had thought to do so. The only lighting was a low-wattage sensor light obscured by tree branches.

Rosie approached the executive committee about investing in a more secure deadlock for the entrance door, better lighting that would be left switched on throughout the night, a tree-lopper to cut back the screening trees and a closed-circuit camera to record all comings and goings through the main door. Rosie presented three quotes to carry out the work, all of which amounted to about $2000. She also offered to monitor the camera herself including changing the tapes and maintaining the equipment.

Rosie's proposal was tabled at the AGM two months later and members discussed the issue. One member complained about the privacy invasion that the camera would impose, another first-floor unit owner expressed that new, brighter lighting would stream unwanted light into her bedroom at night and keep her awake. It was decided by the members at the AGM that the committee would be given the responsibility of approving or not approving this request. Although the committee had the money available in the budget and they could understand Rosie's concerns, four of the five committee members agreed it was too much to spend. They agreed on the tree-lopping and lock but denied the new lighting and camera.

Undeterred, Rosie lobbied committee members individually, convincing 79-year-old Mrs Ferguson that her safety was unnecessarily at risk and Damian, father-of-two, that his children's safety could be in jeopardy. Rosie was unable to convince the chairperson to change his mind, but persuaded Julie in apartment 9 to see her argument.

Through her local Neighbourhood Watch representative Rosie gathered crime statistics from the area that clearly showed that strata properties that had implemented the kind of security measures she was suggesting were 64 per cent less likely to be targeted than those without. With the support of three committee members, Rosie was able to convene an EGM of the executive committee where she presented her arguments again, offered up her evidence from Neighbourhood Watch and, by this time, had found another quote for $200 less. With all this supporting her argument, Rosie was able to convince the committee to endorse the proposal.

Voting

In most states and territories voting is conducted by a show of hands at a meeting. In most situations one unit represents one vote (even where there is a joint tenancy).

A unit owner may also request that a poll be taken in lieu of a show of hands at a meeting. Usually this means that each vote will be recorded on paper and that the votes will be based on the unit owner's entitlement as a proportion of the building, rather than a single vote for a single unit.

A ballot is also available, which usually means that the proposed resolution is sent by post, fax, email or other means to unit owners to vote on without having to formally attend a meeting. The vote is then recorded in writing and returned to the person conducting the ballot. Often it is the best way for a committee to reach a decision without organising and attending a meeting. Table 7.5 shows how voting works across the country.

Table 7.5: voting in bodies corporate, by region

Region	Voting process	Is there one vote per unit?	Is there a maximum number of votes per person?
ACT	Votes are conducted by a show of hands at the meeting unless a poll based on unit entitlement is requested	Yes	One only
NSW	Votes are conducted by a show of hands at a meeting; a poll based on unit entitlement is requested	Yes	No limit except in relation to the original owner/ developer (upon a poll vote)
NT	Votes are conducted by a show of hands at the meeting unless a poll based on unit entitlement is requested	Yes	No limit
Qld	Voting is one vote per unit for ordinary and majority resolutions and can be written or in person. If a poll is requested, then voting is still one vote per unit entitlement. Voting can also be conducted outside of a general meeting	Yes	Based on number of lots owned (if fewer than 20)

Region	Voting process	Is there one vote per unit?	Is there a maximum number of votes per person?
SA	Votes are conducted by a show of hands at the meeting or where requested by a unit holder, a ballot can be conducted between meetings	Yes	No limit
Tas.	Votes are conducted by a show of hands at the meeting unless a poll based on unit entitlement is requested	Yes	No limit
Vic.	Voting is one vote for each unit which is indicated by a show of hands (or another prescribed manner) at a meeting. A unit owner may, before or after the vote is taken for an ordinary resolution, require that a poll be taken based on one vote per unit entitlement*	Yes	No limit
WA	Votes are conducted by a show of hands at the meeting unless a poll based on unit entitlement is requested. A ballot is usually used to vote in council members	Yes	No limit

* In Victoria voting may also be conducted by ballot. A quorum for a ballot can be either 50 per cent of the total votes or 50 per cent of the total unit entitlements and therefore the ballot paper should request that each person voting record both their number of units and their unit entitlement.

Proxies

As mentioned, a proxy is a person appointed to represent another person at a meeting or meetings who has the power to vote on their behalf. Each state and territory has specific regulations when it comes to procedures for proxies, as outlined in table 7.6. In Queensland those who own the management rights for a property (the right to derive income from renting out properties) cannot be a proxy and vote on behalf of owners.

Table 7.6: proxies, by region

Region	Is there a maximum number of proxies that one member can hold?	Must a proxy form be provided with the meeting notice?	What is the latest a proxy can be presented?
ACT	No limit	Yes	N/A
NSW	No limit	Yes	At or before the first meeting to which the proxy relates. In schemes with over 100 unit, 24 hours before meeting
NT	No limit	No	In a unanimous resolution — prior to start of meeting
Qld	If the scheme has more that 20 units, it's 5% of the units. If less than 20, 1 proxy	Yes	Prior to start of meeting
SA	No limit	No	Prior to meeting

Region	Is there a maximum number of proxies that one member can hold?	Must a proxy form be provided with the meeting notice?	What is the latest a proxy can be presented?
Tas.	No limit	No	Prior to start of meeting
Vic.	No limit	Yes, including a statement that they have the right to appoint a proxy	Prior to start of meeting
WA	No limit	No	Prior to start of meeting

Source: Adapted from NCTI. Additional tables and information are available from the National Community Titles Institute website. Visit <www.ncti.org.au>.

Get involved

The best way to make things happen in your body corporate is obviously to get yourself elected onto the executive committee, although there are pros and cons to doing this (see table 7.7). This is a relatively easy task within some bodies corporate where the current members of the executive committee are there under sufferance and because no-one else is prepared to do it. Others are more difficult to infiltrate because of longstanding relationships or reluctance for change. In Victoria, a body corporate with 13 or more units must elect a committee at each AGM. If there are fewer than 13, electing a committee is optional.

Running an effective meeting

If you manage to get yourself elected as chair, you will need to convene and run meetings. Running a successful committee meeting is no different from running any meeting well. Whether it's a meeting of the school fundraising committee, between company departments, between states and territories or between nations, the same principles apply.

Table 7.7: pros and cons of getting involved in your executive committee

Pros	Cons
You can influence what happens in your scheme.	It can be time consuming, depending on the size of the body corporate, your role and what issues arise.
It's a good way to meet your neighbours.	
You will develop a clearer understanding of your body corporate.	It can decrease your popularity among your neighbours when difficult decisions have to be made.
You can gain committee experience (or become an office holder) which might assist in your professional life.	
You can assist in maintaining or enhancing the value of your property.	

Running an effective meeting is all about preparation, processes and protocols. They can be as simple as *everyone gets a chance to speak and all ideas will be considered by the group*, all the way up to a formal agenda with time limits on items and voting on motions.

The following tips will see you through:

1 *Develop the agenda and send it out to committee members at least two weeks before the meeting.* Contact your members a few days before the meeting reminding them of the date,

time and location and requesting any agenda items they would like to see included. Send out copies of anything they need to consider at the meeting such as proposals or quotes for work. Presenting items on the spot and asking members to vote then and there is unfair and members may feel they are being bombarded. Give them time to process information before they are asked to give it their support or otherwise.

2   *Conduct the meeting at a location that suits the style of the committee.* If the committee is small, it is fine to conduct the committee meeting at the home of one of the members. Larger bodies corporate may have access to a designated meeting room or other 'neutral territory' on-site. It's best not to conduct it at a local pub where there will be constant interruptions and run the risk of members not taking it seriously. A quiet location where members can concentrate on the issues is probably best.

3   *Ensure everyone is clear on the ground rules for the meeting.* Ideally these should be developed as a group at the first meeting and include, at a minimum, issues such as respecting people's views and allowing everyone the chance to speak uninterrupted.

4   *Keep track of time.* If you have a full agenda or you know from past experience that your meetings tend to drag on, set a time limit for discussing each issue. You can always revisit that issue if you have time at the end or convene a subcommittee to investigate it further outside the committee meeting. It is the chair's job to keep members focused on the issues at hand and prevent them from veering too much off the track.

5   *Encourage participation.* Not everyone on your executive committee will be an extravert or even very confident about voicing their opinion in front of the group. Make an extra effort to involve these people; they have

as much say as anyone else and may just need a little encouragement.

6   *Review all decisions reached.* At the end of your meeting, ask the secretary to recap all the decisions made or all the actions that have been assigned to individual members (such as seeking quotes for some maintenance work or agreeing that all residents will mow the common lawns on a roster basis).

7   *Try to end on a positive note.* As much as possible, try to ensure that nothing is left unresolved. Ask members if they have any other matters they wish to discuss (time permitting) before you close the meeting. You want your members to leave the meeting feeling that their issues have been given due consideration.

8   *Distribute the minutes.* Circulate the minutes within a week of the meeting. If you leave it too long, members may no longer have a fresh recollection of what was said or agreed. Promptness also comes across as more professional.

Make sure you get agreement at the end of discussions about the course of action you will take. Some issues can be tossed around for what seems like hours without a resolution. Even if a consensus can't be reached, an agreement about how to make progress on the issue to resolution should be documented. This might be something like, 'Reconvene a subgroup comprising Adrian Doheney, Jacinta Coughlan and John Hubbard to review the quotes when they come in and make a decision on option A or option B'.

AGMs are usually required if the body corporate has either received or paid out money within that financial year.

For more tips on running an effective meeting, check out these useful books:

- *Meetings and Event Planning For Dummies,* by Susan Friedmann

- *The Secrets of Facilitation: The SMART Guide to Getting Results With Groups,* by Michael Wilkinson

- *Horsley's Meetings: Procedure, Law and Practice,* 5th Edition, by AD Lang

- *Guide for Meetings and Organisations,* Volume 2, by Nick Renton.

Getting things done

In larger bodies corporate where the activity is more frequent and the workload is greater, it's often a good idea to break up areas into subcommittees. This might include a:

- *building committee* to advise the executive committee on matters concerning capital works, maintenance and repairs to buildings

- *grounds committee* to manage issues related the gardens, landscaping and any outdoor sports facilities such as tennis courts

- *facilities committee* that takes care of the gym, common laundry and any other indoor amenities

- *grievance committee* to hear complaints.

Setting up these subcommittees will hopefully reduce the amount of discussion that needs to happen at a whole-of-group level as the subgroup will hold internal discussions first, reach a consensus and then report back to the committee.

Getting your voice heard

A corrupt (or seriously misguided) executive committee has ways and means of keeping tight control over their little patch of turf. They can block issues from showing up in the minutes, out-and-out refuse to discuss anything contentious by barring it from the agenda (and so that it never ends up in the minutes), and withhold correspondence (read: complaints) so that prospective buyers never see the compaints. They can potentially go on doing this until they have sold up and moved on, leaving the owners who are left behind to deal with the problems. They can do it so long as they are all in cahoots together and have a pact to sit on issues.

These actions, by the way, are against the law. You, as a property owner within the body corporate, can insist on having discussions noted in the minutes and force issues to be added to the agenda. Under the standing orders governing strata properties, the chair (or secretary) may not refuse to add anything to the agenda. If you come up against this, I advise sending them a gentle written reminder of their legal obligations (and copying the letter to all committee members as well as to the strata manager and building manager if they exist).

If you still feel your concerns are not being given the 'airtime' you think they deserve, you can always send another letter outlining what they are. While the committee can refuse to discuss the matter, they cannot legally ignore the existence of the letter. The fact that it has been received must be minuted and filed with official correspondence.

If these actions have still taken you nowhere, it's time to approach your local Office of Fair Trading or consumer affairs bureau (see table 7.8 for the relevant contact in your state or territory). You can register a complaint that your body corporate is not operating according to the law. This complaint, along with the collection of paper you have amassed as evidence of your struggle, should be enough to either get some results or get the committee ejected at the next AGM.

But remember, you won't do yourself any favours or help your case if you act like a raving lunatic throughout this process. Remember to keep your cool and consider the following:

- *Don't single out individual people.* Even if you strongly believe one person is the primary source of the problems, keep your complaint about the committee, not necessarily the shortcomings of an individual. And don't accuse that individual of anything. Keep it about the issues that are not being addressed.

- *Avoid spouting off about conspiracy theories.* You're the only one who will come out of it looking paranoid or, at worse, delusional.

- *Stay on point.* You will only undermine your own credibility if you carry on and on about minor issues. Stick to the major ones. Keep your arguments short and to the point.

Table 7.8: government help to resolve issues with your executive committee, by region

Region	Authority	Website
ACT	Office of Fair Trading	<www.fairtrading.act.gov.au>
NSW	Office of Fair Trading	<www.fairtrading.nsw.gov.au>
NT	Office of Consumer and Business Affairs	<www.caba.nt.gov.au>
Qld	Office of Fair Trading	<www.fairtrading.qld.gov.au>
SA	Office of Consumer and Business Affairs	<www.ocba.sa.gov.au>
Tas.	Consumer Affairs and Fair Trading	<www.consumer.tas.gov.au>
Vic.	Consumer Affairs Victoria	<www.consumer.vic.gov.au>

Table 7.8 *(cont'd)*: government help to resolve issues with your executive committee, by region

Region	Authority	Website
WA	Department of Consumer and Employment Protection	\<www.docep.wa.gov.au\>

If all else fails, take over

The executive committee of a body corporate is set up in the same way as any board or committee in the corporate world. It can wield significant power and it can be toppled. As in any democracy, majority rules, so if you don't support the way your committee is being run, and you can find enough other owners who agree with you, you are completely within your rights to launch a coup. But think this through carefully. Such action is extreme and always unpleasant and you still have to live close to the people you have overturned. Buying a piece of property is the biggest investment most of us will make in our lifetime and, for many, their home is their castle. Many people don't take kindly to being told how to live and losing the power they once had can leave a lot of people feeling very bitter indeed. And what if you lose? How will *you* feel facing up to the people who trounced you?

If you still want to go ahead — having exhausted all attempts to turn the current committee around — here are some things to keep in mind:

- *Be prepared*. Be passionate and be organised. These qualities are your best chances of success. Distribute your 'campaign material' to all owners in the body corporate outlining why they should support you. You should, as anyone campaigning for a leadership position would, outline your 'platform' including your aims, goals, philosophy and vision for the future. If it's a relatively small body corporate, contacting each owner in person will be far more effective. That way, you can discuss their individual issues with them and ask point-blank if you have their support.

- *Stay cool-headed and keep your criticisms professional.* No matter how much owners disagree with their current committee, they are not going to replace them with someone who slings mud and mounts personal attacks on existing members. Keep a level head and remain professional at all times, keeping your arguments about process and the record of the existing executive committee, not personal matters. Don't use your coup attempt as a forum to air personal grievances or for character attacks.

- *Have a potential team ready to go.* If your plan works and you manage to win power, it's a good idea to have a core group of people behind you who are ready to stand for a position on your new committee. There would be nothing worse after all the work you've done to then install a new committee that is just as ineffective as the previous group!

Case study: taking over an executive committee

Hamish felt the executive committee of his high-rise apartment building was completely ineffective, almost to the point of being dysfunctional. His voice had gone unheard at committee meetings because, he felt, he was relatively new to the block and found it difficult to penetrate the 'old boys' group that had run the committee for nearly a decade. No matter how hard he tried, his pleas to have dangerously cracked paving repaired, clearly diseased trees

---

Case study: taking over an executive committee *(cont'd)*

removed and threadbare hallway carpet replaced fell on deaf ears. What's more, his requests were all but ignored in the official AGM minutes.

Feeling he was fighting a losing battle, Hamish planned a coup. Given the number of apartments in the 20-storey block, Hamish made up flyers to drop in all letterboxes. But, on orders from the building manager, the concierge barred Hamish from accessing the residents' letterboxes that were located behind the concierge's desk. Unfazed, Hamish stood in the lobby and distributed his flyers to residents as they came and went. Hamish's flyers encouraged other apartment-owners to contact him if they shared his views. To his surprise, many of them did. With the support of about 40 per cent of the owners, Hamish called an EGM and had the committee ousted—and got to know many of his neighbours in the process.

What next?

One of the most common things you'll rely on your body corporate for is maintenance. Chapter 8 looks at this area in more detail.

Chapter 8

Maintenance

For many people living in a body corporate situation, maintenance is the main thing they are concerned about, mostly because much of it is out of their control.

Buying property is probably the biggest purchase most of us will make in our lifetime. You will want to protect that asset and increase its value by ensuring all maintenance and repairs are carried out properly. A property that looks rundown and in a state of disrepair will never attract as good a price as other more well-looked after properties when the time comes to sell. Sure, if it's a house you can advertise it as a 'renovator's delight', but for strata properties, most people are aware that there will be limits on what they can do. They will probably assume from the look of the place that they will have to fork out for any costs because the body corporate appears to be sitting on its hands.

Of course, in reality, part of the responsibility for maintenance rests with the body corporate and part of it with owners. But how do you distinguish between the two?

Carrying out maintenance work

Every property ages, whether located in a strata scheme or not. With age comes the need for repairs; not only for aesthetic reasons, but also for safety. When you're leaving this up to the body corporate, you want to make sure the repairs are attended to safely and within a reasonable budget. After all, it's your money they're spending.

Any work needs to be carried out by well-credentialed professionals, especially major jobs such as:

- replacing a roof
- repairing a facade
- rectifying concrete splintering
- building fences
- replacing windows
- repairing cracked walls
- waterproofing or dealing with rising damp
- replacing driveways or other concrete areas.

In all states (except Queensland) managers can arrange repairs and maintenance on instruction from the committee or a resolution of the body corporate. In some states there are limits on how much can be spent on repairs without a general meeting decision or special resolution (see table 8.1 for an Australia-wide breakdown).

Maintenance plans

Some states require bodies corporate over a certain size to develop some kind of maintenance plan for the scheme (in Victoria, for example, it applies only to prescribed owners corporations with more than 100 units or an excess of

$200000 in annual fees). The maintenance plan generally covers all planning for future repairs to the buildings and other common property items such as driveways, fences, lifts, air-conditioning, balconies, windows, doors, roofs and the cost of maintaining any garden areas.

Table 8.1: requirements for carrying out repairs and maintenance, by region

Region	Can managers carry out maintenance on behalf of a scheme?	Do monetary limitations apply to repair spending?	What is the maximum amount per unit for improvements or maintenance?
ACT	Yes	No	N/A
NSW	Yes	Yes (in large schemes)	None (in schemes with over 100 units it's the budget amount plus 10%. Two quotes required)
NT	Yes	Yes (only budgeted amount without special resolution)	Unlimited
Qld	No	Yes (committee limits apply)	No limit for maintenance. Two quotes needed if over $250 per unit; special resolution if over $300 per unit
SA	Yes	Yes	Special resolution required if over $5000 per unit

Table 8.1 *(cont'd)*: requirements for carrying out repairs and maintenance, by region

Region	Can managers carry out maintenance on behalf of a scheme?	Do monetary limitations apply to repair spending?	What is the maximum amount per unit for improvements or maintenance?
Tas.	Yes	No	N/A
Vic.	Yes	No	N/A
WA	Yes	Yes; $65 per unit	Unlimited (if in budget); $65 per unit as prescribed in regulations

Source: Adapted from NCTI. Additional tables and information are available from the National Community Titles Institute website. Visit <www.ncti.org.au>.

The maintenance plan will usually set out the major capital items that will need to be repaired or replaced within the next 10 years. For each of those items, it will usually need to stipulate:

- their present condition
- an estimated time frame for the repair or replacement
- an estimated cost
- the estimated life of the item once repaired.

A maintenance plan can be developed 'in-house' or by an external consultant. If you're thinking of engaging a consultant, table 8.2 gives some hints as to what to consider. Once adopted, the maintenance plan will need to be reported on at each AGM.

Table 8.2: the dos and don'ts of outsourced maintenance plans

Do	Don't
Review your situation and what you are trying to achieve. Do you want the bare minimum report or a blueprint for improving your property? Are you considering only maintenance of existing items or do you want to add to the amenity of the property? Would you also like an 'eco audit'? The 'effective' lifespan of plant and equipment can be very different if ecological issues are considered.	Don't pay peanuts and expect a premium result.
	Don't rush things. A properly considered report specific to your requirements, your brief, your building and your situation (and including all the results of a physical inspection of the property) will take more than a day to organise.
Consider whether you can do it yourself or should engage expert assistance.	Don't engage a consultant only on a word-of-mouth recommendation. Conduct your own investigations.
Choose the right consultant:	Don't accept a report that appears inadequate — follow through and ask questions.
Are they appropriate for your needs and situation? The consultant who is right for a four-unit walk-up may not be appropriate for a 20-storey high-rise with significant building defects.	Don't use the report as the sole input to your funding decision; the scope of work and how to fund it are totally separate decisions. A good maintenance plan is only one of a number of relevant issues to consider when making funding decisions.
Are they are a member of the relevant professional association?	
Are they a member of the state strata institute?	
Do they have the appropriate qualifications?	
Do they carry the appropriate insurance?	

Table 8.2 *(cont'd)*: the dos and don'ts of outsourced maintenance plans

Do	Don't
Will a qualified and experienced person do a thorough physical inspection or is it only a 'desk report'? Brief the consultant properly. Make sure you know what they intend to do and that they know what you are trying to achieve. Recognise that this is a plan for future capital works, *not* a budget for fees. How best to fund the required and desired capital works is always a separate decision requiring separate analysis.	Don't expect your strata manager to do the assessment—they are unlikely to be qualified or trained for this type of work, or to carry the right insurances. Don't let the report sit on the shelf. You will get the most benefit when it becomes part of a dynamic plan for the future of your property.

Maintenance funding

Having a plan for anticipated major capital expenditure is critical. But make sure you don't put the cart before the horse — the maintenance plan comes first! Only after working out the optimum amount to invest in your property should you turn your attention to how best to fund the required or desired capital works.

There are three ways to fund anticipated capital works in a body corporate:

1 maintenance (or sinking) funds

2 special fees/levies

3 borrowing.

Each of these forms of funding has advantages and disadvantages and owners in strata schemes should consider which method (or combination of methods) is best for their particular situation. Criteria that owners should consider when considering their funding options include cost, availability, timing, complexity/ease of use, and understanding and suitability for all owners.

Saving in a maintenance fund can be a good idea (though it's important for owners to remember that it's not compulsory to raise a levy or fee for a maintenance or sinking fund). Like other forms of strata funding, maintenance funds have their advantages and their place in the mix of funding, but often owners are unaware of the costs and disadvantages of this form of funding. Sinking funds are usually more expensive than special levies or borrowing and saving over a long period of time is probably not appropriate if the project should be commenced now.

Special levies are financially very efficient and often the lowest cost method of funding. The problem with them is usually the timing — they can come in lumps and you often can't control when. If you need to fix the garage door of a house, you might choose to wait until after Christmas when you expect to have some more cash. However, in a body corporate, if the garage door needs fixing, it often needs fixing now and so you might get the levy notice at an inconvenient time.

In some ways, borrowing is like a sinking fund in reverse. You get the work done now and you pay for it over time, compared with paying over time for the work to be done later. The good things about borrowing include availability and cost (surprisingly, it's often cheaper than a sinking fund). It's also usually easy to arrange. The bad thing is that you have to pay it back, with interest!

When considering funding options, one of the important things to do is to compare apples with apples when it comes to cost. The body corporate should work out the true cost of the sinking fund. Compare this with the advantages and disadvantages of a special levy and of borrowing. If the body corporate is considering borrowing there should be a calculation of the full interest rate by property, incorporating all fees and charges associated with the loan.

Regular maintenance and repairs aside, if a body corporate wants to significantly upgrade or renovate common property the work must either have been previously listed in the maintenance plan or approved by a special resolution (discussed in chapter 5). 'Significant work' is usually considered anything that will cost more than twice the total amount of annual fees or that requires a council permit. A special resolution is not usually required if the work is considered urgent because of safety concerns or to prevent further major damage.

Value in strata property

Think of the things that make an investment in a house appreciate. Enhanced value in houses usually comes from three areas: economic conditions (the value of all properties appreciates); demographic factors (your local area becomes more or less attractive to purchasers); and capital improvements (you renovate and improve the property, thus enhancing its value).

The concepts are the same in strata, but with one important addition. Economic conditions and demographic factors have pretty much the same impact. Also, you can refurbish the inside of your unit to make it more valuable. However, there's a fourth source of value: the common property.

When someone refurbishes or renovates their house, they will probably look at the entire property and work out where best to invest their time, effort and money. But in a body corporate, you are responsible for inside the unit and the body corporate is responsible for the common property. That is, you only have direct control over one aspect of the renovations. You can make significant improvements to the outside of your strata unit by looking at the common property, typically, the areas between the front gate and your front door. But, of course, to do this, you have to work with and through the body corporate.

Many investors (and also many owner occupiers) don't get the increase in value that they should because they ignore the state of one of the most important aspects of their investment, the common property. Taking an interest in the state of the common property, keeping it well maintained, improving it where it makes sense, taking part in general meetings and contributing via membership of committees are excellent ways to increase the value of your investment.

Maintaining your own unit

Owners are required to maintain the outward appearance of their own units, usually including maintaining eaves and guttering. If you don't, the body corporate in some states has the right to issue you with a written request which, if unfulfilled, can allow them to carry out the work themselves and charge it to you.

As mentioned previously, cosmetic renovations to the inside of your unit are usually at your discretion unless the planned work is significant enough to require a council permit.

Case study: the cost of failing to maintain common property

In November 2006 the New South Wales Supreme Court awarded $150 000 against a body corporate that failed to properly maintain its common property.

Case study: the cost of failing to maintain common property (cont'd)

The case revolved around a top-floor residential unit in North Sydney with an uncovered external terrace. Problems with the waterproof membrane between a concrete slab and the terrace's tiled surface meant that water was able to seep through into the unit. This also caused the terrace's steel frame to rust.

The tenant vacated the property believing it to be unsafe and its owner, Seiwa Australia, began legal action against the body corporate, saying they had breached their responsibility to maintain common property under section 62 of the New South Wales *Strata Schemes Management Act 1996*.

Siewa claimed they had alerted the body corporate to the problem as early as March 2003. The body corporate took no action until the legal case was mounted against them in August 2005.

The court had to decide whether the membrane was actually considered common property and then determine whether a breach had occurred.

The body corporate argued that the terrace was not common property but, because the defect was below the floor's surface, the court found that the problem in question was in fact located in common property. The body corporate also tried to claim that the tenant had contributed to the defect but, again, the court found against the body corporate saying that contributory negligence is no defence against their legal obligations to properly maintain the property.

The court found the body corporate had been aware of the problem but had done nothing to fix it and awarded Seiwa $150 000 based on lost rent while the unit was empty.

> This was a landmark case for bodies corporate in Australia and highlights the importance of clarifying what is common property when registering the strata plan and attending to repairs as quickly as possible.
>
> The body corporate appealed the decision but was unsuccessful.

What next?

Whenever people are living in close proximity to one another disagreements are bound to arise. Chapter 9 looks at resolving disputes in a strata scheme environment.

Chapter 9

Resolving disputes

With some property owners investing a significant amount of time, energy and passion into their home or investment — and the need for the body corporate to run the strata scheme purely as a business — it's no wonder disputes arise from time to time. Sometimes disputes result from safety concerns (such as the 'Rosie' case study in chapter 7), sometimes it's pride in the scheme's appearance, and sometimes it's purely a question of who pays. Whatever the cause, these are all issues that can get some owners pretty fired up and, when you think that for many people their home is their sanctuary, it's often with good reason. Still, the executive committee has a responsibility to all unit owners and has to make socially and economically responsible decisions that consider the sometimes competing interests of everyone. An investor, for example, may not want to spend money on purely cosmetic renovations to a property, whereas a long-term owner–occupier can more clearly see the benefit. Disputes will always come up; the trick is in how to manage them.

Common disputes

In a body corporate situation, disputes will usually arise either between unit owners, owner–occupiers and the body corporate, or between an owner/the body corporate and a neighbour. The most common owner-to-owner disputes tend to be over noise, lack of appropriate maintenance of their own property, or the use of common property (such as constantly parking a car in a common area). Owner–body corporate disputes are commonly over maintenance issues or fees. Body corporate versus neighbour issues can be over anything from overhanging trees to construction noise.

The first steps

Larger bodies corporate will often have an internal dispute or grievance resolution process documented and many dispute-resolving tribunals expect the parties to go through such an internal process before the tribunal will consider reviewing the issue. In Tasmania, the delineation between common and private property is usually so clearcut that any disagreements rarely escalate outside the body corporate. In Western Australia, about 95 per cent of cases are either dismissed or withdrawn by consent.

Formal dispute resolution processes vary from state to state, but the road to them should be universal. The best way to deal with a dispute, if possible, is to not let it get out of hand in the first place. Good communication is vital.

Talk it over

It's amazing how often people who are involved in a dispute have not sat down together to discuss the issue calmly. Some people are inclined to go into battle at the first sign of trouble rather than actually approaching the people with whom they're in dispute and putting forward their case.

Resolving disputes amicably often relies on both sides making some concessions. Listen to the other side's point of view, respect it and see if you can't come to an arrangement that will suit you both. Going in for all or nothing is no way to resolve a disagreement in a civil community.

Dealing with difficult people

No matter what you do, some people will remain difficult. How they act is beyond your control, but you do have a choice when it comes to how you respond to them. People can be influenced by the responses they receive and some will push you to your limit. This is when it's important to set boundaries on their unacceptable behaviour.

Give yourself time to choose your reactions. Flying off the handle won't solve anything and will, in fact, probably enrage (or satisfy!) the prickly person even more. Some ways you can diffuse anger in people is to do the following:

- Let them get their point across. Some people just want to be heard and feel as if they are being understood.

- Step back from the situation while you both cool down. A night's sleep can do wonders to shed new light on a situation.

It's important to realise that the situation is probably not personal. Difficult people tend to be that way with everyone. It might help to try to understand where the person's behaviour is stemming from — often it's a position of fear. Getting to know someone better might help you understand this fear and go part way to brokering a solution.

If no concurrence can be reached, the next step in resolving an owner-to-owner dispute is through the body corporate.

Case study: reaching a compromise

Rick, a young songwriter, spent most of his days sitting at his keyboard composing jingles for advertising campaigns and songs to sell to record companies. Given that he lived in an inner-city low-rise apartment block, the noise he created had never been an issue because most of the other residents were out at work during the day and so there was no-one around to complain. That was until Lena moved in next door.

Lena was a mother of two young children, both of whom were terrible sleepers. They had become particularly unsettled since moving into their new home and the noise from Rick's keyboard only made matters worse. Lena asked Rick if he could turn down the volume, which he did, but the problem remained. Unfortunately, Rick's music room and the children's bedroom shared a wall and no matter how low he kept the noise level, it still disturbed their sleep. Having screaming kids next door didn't do much for Rick's creative concentration either.

On Lena's suggestion, Rick then agreed to try not to play his music between 1.00 pm and 3.00 pm. But that didn't work out either. When he had a deadline, he had a deadline. He had to work and told Lena that she would just have to live with it. Lena, who was tired and frustrated, took her complaint to the chairperson of the executive committee, suggesting he convene a meeting to discuss the issue.

'Why don't you just ask Rick to invest in a pair of headphones?', the chairperson suggested. 'Better yet, why don't you two split the cost?'

It suddenly all seemed so simple. Lena approached Rick with the idea and he agreed.

Problem solved.

Get the body corporate involved

Taking your dispute to a meeting is the next relatively contained way of reaching a resolution. It's important that this step is a mutual decision between both parties and that both will accept the resolution suggested by the body corporate as final.

If the dispute is over a by-law, the body corporate can issue a written notice to the recalcitrant tenant/owner. If the breach is not rectified, the body corporate may then impose fines through the state-based tribunal, Office of Fair Trading or consumer affairs bureau (see appendix D for a state-by-state list of these government authorities).

Of course, if your dispute is *with* the body corporate, the next step is mediation.

Mediation

Mediation is a process used more and more frequently by the legal system as a first resort for dispute resolution. It is favoured for the potential time and cost savings achieved by not dragging a frivolous or straightforward dispute though the courts.

Mediation is the process whereby a neutral or independent moderator assists the quarrelling parties to reach their own solution. It is a relatively inexpensive process (you only pay the mediator for their time) and can be accessed through your state/territory-based consumer authority or through the legal system (see appendix D). It is important to remember that this process is not legally binding, but is made in good faith.

The mediator's role is to:

- help both parties to understand and clarify the issues in dispute
- assist the parties to find ways to address the disagreement

↳ create an environment where both parties can come up with a means of settling the dispute that is acceptable.

Case study: keeping the air fair

Rob, in unit six, decided to install a reverse-cycle air-conditioner in his unit without consulting the body corporate. Because he considered the air-conditioner to be an internal addition to his home he didn't think he needed approval.

It wasn't long before complaints about the air-conditioner came in from neighbours. Some said it was noisy and interrupted their sleep, others said the back of the system jutting out of one of Rob's external walls (facing a common driveway) was an eyesore. A number of residents demanded that the air-conditioner be removed at Rob's expense. Given that the air-conditioner protruded from an external wall, which was part of common property, residents complained directly to the body corporate for resolution.

The body corporate issued a letter to Rob noting that he had breached the by-laws and requested a meeting to discuss how they could remedy the situation. At the meeting, the body corporate suggested that, rather than getting rid of the air-conditioner all together, Rob should move it to another part of the unit (preferably a wall facing his backyard) to limit noise near other units and restore the look of the side wall. Rob refused. After spending $2000 on the system and another $500 having it installed, Rob wanted to keep it in the part of his unit where it was going to be most effective.

The body corporate had no choice then but to issue a letter demanding that Rob remove the air-conditioner. If he did not do so within 28 days, the letter said, the body corporate would organise a tradesperson to remove the system and charge the cost of the job back to Rob.

Rob immediately applied to his state dispute resolution tribunal to settle the matter, feeling the body corporate's internal process had failed him. Unfortunately for Rob, given that he had clearly broken body corporate law by installing an unauthorised appliance in a common property area, the tribunal found in favour of the body corporate, forcing Rob to remove the air-conditioner at his own expense.

Adjudication

In some states, including New South Wales, there is an extra step in the process here: adjudication. Adjudicators usually hear disputes related to issues such as repairs, water penetration, unapproved parking, unapproved pets, noise and alterations to common properties (such as closing in balconies). In this process, both parties make submissions to the independent adjudicator and a decision is returned within about 10 weeks. The parties do not need to appear before anyone as they do in mediation. The adjudicators ruling (and reasons behind it) are then sent back to all parties in writing. An adjudicator's decision is legally binding but dissatisfied parties can appeal to the relevant tribunal. In Tasmania, the Recorder of Titles settles strata scheme disputes and may or may not request a hearing.

Tribunal hearings

The next step, in most Australian states and territories, is to apply to a government-run tribunal for help. In Victoria, this is VCAT (Victorian Civil and Administrative Tribunal) and in Western Australia it is the State Administrative Tribunal (see table 9.1 for state-by-state listing). These authorities make legally binding decisions about how disputes are to be settled.

Tribunals are run like mini courts with similar protocols and processes, although not quite as formal. Generally, solicitors are not required and the parties usually argue their case by themselves. Applications can be made online and submissions must include all information relevant to the case. Tribunal rulings include:

- ordering someone to do something or stop doing something

- imposing a financial penalty for breaking a rule

- ordering damages to be paid to the successful party

- varying a contract or specifying that the contract is now void

- appointing or removing a manager, chairperson or secretary

- appointing an administrator.

Table 9.1: formal dispute resolution processes, by region

Region	Step 1	Step 2	Step 3	Step 4
ACT*	Internal dispute resolution	Magistrate's Court	Supreme Court	
NSW	Mediation	Application to the Strata Schemes Adjudicator	Application to the Consumer, Trader and Tenancy Tribunal	Office of Fair Trading
NT	Internal dispute resolution	Local Court—small claims jurisdiction		

Region	Step 1	Step 2	Step 3	Step 4
Qld	Self-resolution	Commissioner for Body Corporate and Community Management (mediation and conciliation)	Commissioner for Body Corporate and Community Management (adjudication)	District Court
SA	Community mediation services	Office of Consumer and Business Affairs	Magistrate's Court	
Tas.	Body corporate's internal dispute resolution process	The Recorder of Titles ('The Recorder')	Resource Management and Planning Appeal Tribunal (for appeals)	
Vic.	Internal dispute resolution	Conciliation through Consumer Affairs	Application to VCAT	Magistrate's Court
WA	State Administrative Tribunal (mediation)	State Administrative Tribunal (compulsory conference)	State Administrative Tribunal (final hearing)	

* This process was under review at the time of writing, with plans to establish a civil and arbitration tribunal in the ACT. The ACT Planning and Land Authority (ACT PLA) is currently the agency that handles disputes involving builders and developers.

A state-by-state breakdown of dispute resolution processes can be found at appendix B. Contact details are provided in appendix D.

What next?

So you've decided to sell up. What do you need to think about when it comes to selling a strata property? Chapter 10 ties it all together for you.

Chapter 10

Selling up

There are many reasons why you might sell a unit. It might be a financial decision (particularly for an investor); you might want to move to a different neighbourhood, into a bigger place or out of a strata situation all together. Whatever the motivation, you want to ensure your property is presented in its best light to attract buyers and that all your body corporate fees are in order before you go (so there are no nasty surprises after you've moved).

If you're on your body corporate's executive committee, it means you can help make sure the external appearance of the scheme is up to scratch. If you're not involved, you will have less say and that may affect the value of your unit. I said it before and I'll say it again: it pays to be on the executive committee. You must, however, act in good faith and therefore in the best interests of the members of the body corporate.

Preparing your unit

Most of us don't live in homes that you might find gracing the pages of *Home Beautiful*. Our homes are decorated in our own style, which might not appeal to everyone. Most real estate agents are great about telling you what they think is worth doing to improve your unit's presentation for sale. After all, it's in their best interests to get the maximum price for the property as well.

The big thing real estate agents talk about these days is that you're selling a 'lifestyle', not just a unit. That means you want your property to appeal to a certain type of buyer. If potential buyers of your place are people that will want a low-maintenance property, make it appear that way by simplifying the garden. De-clutter to give the place the appearance of being easy to clean.

Stand firm on your advertising budget. Some agents will say you need the biggest, brightest board on the front lawn and full-page ads in every newspaper for the duration of your selling campaign. Consider whether you think this is necessary given most people search for properties online these days (the most inexpensive component of your marketing campaign) and make sure the body corporate is happy to let you erect the size of sign you want in the location you want. Perhaps half-page ads in the local real estate guide will be enough and if you live on a main road with lots of exposure, the elaborate sign with four internal photos may not really be necessary.

Real estate agents are the experts. In most cases I would advise you to let them choose which features to highlight in the advertising material. They know the market and know what buyers tend to look for.

There is no limit to how much you can spend on your home pre-sale. Some owners will re-carpet, re-polish floors and even rent furniture to make their unit more appealing. Give your agent a budget that you're prepared to spend and listen to their advice about what's worth doing and what's not. From my experience, there are a number of things that are definitely worth doing:

- *De-clutter.* This is the first thing most agents will tell you to do. You want to give the illusion of space and units that are packed to the rafters with junk don't do that. Make the most of the unit's best features and downplay the not-so-great features. This means taking unnecessary items off your kitchen bench (such as kettles, toasters, even microwave if necessary) to make it seem as if there's more bench space.

- *Clean up.* I know this sounds obvious but a tidy unit is important. It's tempting to think that buyers will look beyond the crumbs on the kitchen floor and the hair in the sink, but some can't. They might translate your lack of cleanliness to you not caring about the unit and assume you haven't taken good care of it while you were there.

- *Tidy behind the scenes.* Conducting an open for inspection is not like opening up your home for a dinner party. Dinner party guests are unlikely to open drawers and cupboards so it's okay to shove things behind anything that closes. Buyers will potentially open every cupboard, wardrobe and drawer so making them neat inside will give a better impression.

- *Re-paint.* If the place is looking a little tired or the walls have more cracks than a Chinese vase, fill them in and repaint. A new coat of paint is a relative inexpensive way to give any home a fresh look. If you're going to the trouble of painting, choose light, neutral colours that won't close in the space; dark colours on the walls and ceiling tend to make a room feel smaller.

- *Tidy the garden.* If you don't want to go to the extent of buying flowering plants to brighten up the yard, at least weed and apply some mulch to make it look tidy. If you have lawn that you are responsible for maintaining, make sure it is mowed. Neat edges also make a big difference. Trim scraggly branches and plants away from windows to let more light into the unit.

Strata funding and your sales return

It's worth taking a moment to cover some of the financial issues that might come into play when you sell your unit. Sensible purchasers should take into consideration all the relevant financial issues of the body corporate including, for example, anticipated or special levies, the current and future amount of ongoing levies, and any borrowings the body corporate might have. Of course, if your body corporate has borrowed funds, then the repayments will be reflected in the ongoing levies for which the purchaser is responsible.

Let's take a simple case and assume the capital works were done and paid for yesterday and you sell the unit today. First of all, the value of your unit has increased because of the capital works done on the common property — the method of funding doesn't impact this. If the body corporate funded the works using funds in a sinking fund, then you need to include your contributions to the fund in working out your net return from the sale. The benefit you get from the sale isn't simply the amount the purchaser pays — you have to reduce this by your sinking fund contributions.

If the work was funded with a special levy, then you need to adjust the sale price by the amount of the special levy to work out your net return. That is, your net return is the price the purchaser pays less the amount of the special levy. If the works on the common property were funded by a loan, then the purchaser should take this into account when considering the offer price.

Whether the capital works on the property were funded by savings in the sinking fund, a special levy or borrowing, your net return should be approximately the same.

Ways to sell

How you go about selling your unit—whether by private sale/treaty, auction or on your own—is probably a decision best made with a real estate agent. They will be best placed to know what the market is doing and, judging by the attributes of your individual property and the buyers it's likely to attract, what is the best method of sale. As mentioned in chapter 5, there are pros and cons for each, so getting professional advice is your best bet.

Choosing a real estate agent

Let's face it: real estate agents are a dime a dozen and will never refuse to list a property for sale. They all want your business and, in most areas, there are many to choose from. But how do you choose? Table 10.1 offers some tips.

Table 10.1: the dos and don'ts of choosing a real estate agent

Do	Don't
Check whether they are a member of the respective real estate institute in your state or territory.	Don't be bowled over by slick marketing spiels.
Ask them to discuss the ethical standards they work by.	Don't be dazzled by the agent who quotes you the highest price. If you think what they're quoting is excessive, ask them to commit to it in writing and ask if they're willing to forego their commission if it doesn't reach that price.
Check whether they have a good knowledge of the local property market.	
Ask them to explain their proposed marketing strategy and how they intend to keep you updated on their progress.	

Table 10.1 *(cont'd)*: the dos and don'ts of choosing a real estate agent

Do	Don't
Ask friends and neighbours for recommendations. Knock on the door of houses that have recently been sold and ask what the owner thought of their agent.	Don't limit yourself to the agents who seem to have the most 'for sale' signs up in your area. Yes, they may have a lot of experience, but some of the smaller operators might give you more personalised service or spend more time marketing your property for you (and working harder for their commission!).
Make sure you understand all costs including their all-important commission. This will be expressed as a percentage of the sale price. Ensure it is competitive.	
Understand the agreement they want you to sign. Most will want an exclusive contract meaning that you are not able to sign with another agent to sell that unit within a certain time frame (even if you are completely unhappy with their service). The contracts will also often detail a maximum marketing spend; take note of what that is and challenge it if you feel it's too high.	
Most importantly, go with your gut instinct. If you don't feel comfortable with the agent, don't go with them (make sure it's the agent you're not comfortable with, not the idea of selling your beloved unit!).	

Case study: choosing your real estate agent carefully

Tania and Tony decided to sell their much-loved villa unit in order to move closer to Tony's children who lived on the other side of town. They were keen to get their home sold before Christmas so they could relax over the festive break.

Tania and Tony met a few local real estate agents who all seemed to have slightly different ways of approaching the selling process but all of whom appeared to have a good understanding of the local market. Some promised they could achieve a certain price at auction; others were more conservative in their estimations.

With very little difference between them, Tania and Tony had trouble deciding which agent to sign with. They settled on one who, although they felt was a little slippery, seemed to have achieved good sales in the area recently and had many years' experience in their neighbourhood.

Within two weeks of signing the contract, Tania and Tony were already unhappy with the lack of service they were experiencing. The agent was slow to return phone calls, slow to organise the marketing material they had discussed and had committed their money to an over-the-top advertising campaign that Tania and Tony felt was completely unnecessary. When they tried to protest, the agent pointed out that they had agreed to a maximum advertising spend in their contract, even though the agent had told them they probably wouldn't need to spend that much at the time of signing.

Tania and Tony were furious and told the agent they wanted to fire him and end the contract. That was fine, the agent said, but reminded them that because they had signed an exclusive 60-day contract, they would not be able to sign up another agent to sell their unit for about another 45 days. That would mean they would never be able to sell their unit by Christmas. Tania and Tony were left wondering what to do.

Case study: working with others to make improvements

Tom and Cath live in a 1990s apartment block in Brisbane and they're ready to sell, but they're unsure of how much they should spend on improvements. Their city apartment block comprises four floors of residential and two floors of commercial space.

Over the 12 years that Tom and Cath have lived in the apartment, they have found that the needs of all the owners have varied considerably, requiring frequent compromises to meet everyone's building requests. Tom himself has been quite proactive, initiating and responding to a number of suggestions to improve the building's value in different ways and getting himself elected to the executive committee.

Soon after moving in, Tom discovered that the balcony railings were two centimetres short of the current requirements under the building code of Australia. In addition, the horizontal rails could be used as a ladder by a child allowing them to climb up and possibly fall over the top of the railing. He wisely saw this as an unacceptable risk. He made an application to the executive committee to have the railings changed to include a new chrome rail with a glass infill panel below. Although the residents were happy with the proposal, the businesses on the first two floors felt the proposed building materials were too costly and requested a cheaper option be considered. This was understandable given they would get no direct benefit from the residential balconies.

Tom managed to convince them that the proposed railing would modernise the outward appearance of the whole block which would benefit them too. The committee approved the work, using the sinking fund as it was a capital non-recurrent cost.

The decision paid off for the businesses because when the time came to replace the air-conditioning system on their floors, the residential owners agreed to help fund the upgrade and the committee passed the request.

Being part of the executive committee and allowing for some give and take paid dividends when the time came for Tom and Cath to sell; the modern look of the building attracted a much higher price than what they had originally paid.

Settling up before you go

Just because you are leaving a body corporate, it doesn't mean you can skip out of paying all the fees you owe up until the time you leave. An adjustment will be made at the time the property settles ensuring your fees are paid up until that date.

A final word from the author

It doesn't take a genius to work out that body corporate law and regulations are complicated, especially when you're trying to cover the myriad rules across the country in one text. I wanted to create a resource that would be useful to body corporate owners and tenants around the country. I wanted to equip people with the tools to help them better understand how bodies corporate work and, in doing that, make their lives that little bit easier... and happier.

I also wanted to inspire people to continue to invest their money — and lives — into strata property. I hope I've managed to do that. I hope I've convinced you that the future is bright for strata schemes. Urban planning policies around the country are targeting annual growth of more than 10 per cent over the next 10 to 15 years, so expect to see more and more strata schemes popping up all over the country. As with all properties, the value of strata properties will continue to go up; in some cities, such as Adelaide and Hobart in 2007, at an even faster rate than houses. And, with our ageing population, there really has never been a better time to invest in this kind of property.

In the commercial market we're seeing more mixed-use developments where shops line the ground floor of high- or low-rise apartment blocks with residential units on the floors above. With land availability constantly decreasing in our cities, this is the obvious answer for city planners and developers — to start building our homes towards the sky.

I have done my best to give you the most accurate and up-to-date information I can throughout this book. But with one piece of strata legislation or another constantly under review somewhere around the country (at the time of writing New South Wales, Queensland and the ACT all had strata law reforms in progress) it has been difficult, but I've had a lot of help from the people I've mentioned in the acknowledgements and contributors pages.

If it hasn't been made clear enough already, I love strata living and I hope, armed with the information contained in this book, you too will enjoy it for years to come. And remember, if you need any help, drop me a line at <stephen.r@acebodycorp.com.au>. I'm always happy to point you in the right direction.

Stephen Raff

administrative fund: The pool of money managed by the executive committee used to cover all recurring day-to-day expenses of the body corporate such as the cost of maintaining common property, paying insurance premiums and any other recurrent funds not covered by either the sinking fund, a special levy or borrowing.

annual general meeting (AGM): The yearly meeting of the body corporate convened by the manager or executive committee to which all the unit owners are invited. All unit owners must also be invited to the first AGM where the original owner/developer hands over all relevant papers and votes are cast on issues such as insurance and determining rules/by-laws. The executive committee is also elected at the first AGM and following yearly meetings.

body corporate: Commonly referred to as an 'owners corporation' in recent legislation, a body corporate is the legal entity with responsibility for managing the common property within a strata scheme.

by-laws: The rules that apply to an individual strata scheme as determined by the body corporate.

caretaker/building manager: Person employed by the body corporate to help manage the strata scheme. Responsibilities typically include overseeing common property maintenance.

common property: Areas within a strata scheme that are shared by unit owners and managed by the body corporate, such as lawns and gardens, driveways, hallways or lifts.

company title: A company is formed for the purpose of owning a property consisting of more than one dwelling and its constitution provides that its shares held in groups entitle the holder to use and occupy a specified unit at the property. The company operates under company law.

dummy bidding: Dummy bids are fake bids made at an auction by attendees with no real intent to buy the property. These bids are placed in an attempt to artificially inflate the price of a property, usually to mislead or deceive potential buyers. This practice is illegal in Australia.

executive committee: The group of elected owners (or their representatives) who are responsible for running and maintaining the strata scheme. They will usually comprise between two and 12 members, depending on this size of the scheme.

First Home Owner Grant (FHOG): Federal government scheme introduced in July 2000 originally to offset the effect of the GST on home ownership. It's a one-off grant payable to first homeowners who satisfy all the eligibility criteria. It is funded through each state and territory and administered under their own legislation.

levies: Contributions paid by owners to the body corporate to cover expenditure. These are usually paid quarterly and the amount is based on unit entitlement (or, in Victoria, lot liability). The term is used interchangeably with 'fees' in this book.

lot: See 'unit'.

owner–occupier: A person who owns the property they live in.

owners corporation: See 'body corporate'.

plan of subdivision: See 'strata plan'. Plan that stipulates which components of a strata scheme are privately owned and which are common property.

proxy: A person appointed to represent another person at a meeting or meetings. The proxy is authorised to vote on behalf of the person they represent.

quorum: The number of members required to be present at a meeting to make decisions binding. In a body corporate, this is usually half the members but in some states it is one-quarter of the people entitled to vote (or owners entitled to vote owning one-quarter of the units). If the block consists of only two units, the quorum is both. In an executive committee, it is usually half the members.

resident: A person who lives within a strata scheme but does not necessarily own the unit (they might be renting).

sinking fund: One of the three forms of funding anticipated major capital expenditure. A sinking fund is a type of savings fund in which unit owners make regular deposits to be used later for a specific purpose such as unforeseen major repairs. As with the other forms of funding, sinking funds have advantages and disadvantages that should be considered when determining the best method of funding future capital expenditure in your situation.

special levy: Another of the forms of funding major capital works. A special levy is a fee charged to unit owners to pay for a one-off item that will benefit all owners. It may be to buy new equipment or be introduced to cover an unforeseen legal requirement. As with a sinking fund, it also has advantages and disadvantages that should be considered when deciding an appropriate form of funding (or mix of funding) for your situation.

strata management plan: A document that sets out the way a building will operate when sharing with areas that are not part of the same strata scheme, such as retail areas or areas that contain a number of apartment blocks, all on different schemes. The plan defines how the whole complex will work together including governance and cost sharing.

strata manager: Also referred to as a managing agent (or owners corporation/body corporate manager), this is a company that is appointed by a majority vote of the body corporate or the committee to manage the strata scheme. Its responsibilities are defined by the body corporate (or committee) but often include administration, record keeping, tax and legal matters, dispute resolution and overseeing maintenance.

strata plan: Plan that stipulates which components of a strata scheme are privately owned and which are common property. May go under other names depending where you are in Australia.

strata property: See 'unit'.

strata scheme: Refers to the collection of units overseen by the body corporate.

strata title: Land title that specifically covers strata properties.

tenant: Person who lives in a unit leased from its owner.

unit: The individual apartments, flats, townhouses or other privately owned areas within a body corporate. Also referred to as 'strata properties' or 'lots' and can apply equally to commercial properties.

vendor: Person who owns a property that is up for sale.

What's yours and what's common property?

Around Australia, the term 'common property' usually refers to shared facilities such as central driveways, landscaping, hallways, staircases and lifts. There are state- and territory-specific exceptions (as outlined below), but to be sure you should always consult your body corporate's individual strata plan.

Australian Capital Territory

In the ACT, common property differs between A- and B-class developments. Common property is not different in any type of development whether it is commercial, mixed use or high-rise residential. Invariably, high-rise residential developments are A-class. However, if the high-rise is a three-storey townhouse development with all units attached, but no titles are above each other (that is, one owner has all three levels), then this is generally a B-class development. Mixed developments of high-rise and townhouse apartments are generally A-class, although there are some older types of developments that are a mix of both A- and B-class. In those older developments, the owners have resolved by way of a special resolution that they will be deemed to be A-class for the purpose of repair and maintenance.

A-class units

A-class units are defined as a unit with the boundaries of that unit being midway between the walls, floors and ceiling. A-class units often have 'unit subsidiaries' annexed to the unit. For example, courtyards, storage areas, balconies, parking areas and garages.

In an A-class development, the common property is anything that is an external area of the building such as external walls, windows, the roof and, of course, things like stairwells, corridors, pools, spas, grounds, gym, tennis courts, paths and parking areas.

The *Unit Titles Act 2001* requires that in an A-class development the owners corporation be responsible for the structural integrity of load-bearing parts or 'defined parts' of the building, such as balconies, walls, columns, footings, slabs and beams.

So, if there is some form of leakage on the balcony, then the owners corporation must undertake that repair (even though it is within the unit subsidiary), as failure to do so may result in concrete cancer that, in turn, would affect the structural integrity of the balcony. The repair and maintenance of any tiling affixed to the balcony is generally considered to be the responsibility of the unit owner, as that is aesthetic and can be applied and changed at any time at the whim of the owner, and has no impact on the structural integrity of the balcony.

It could be that a pool is constructed on a suspended slab above an underground parking area. If, for example, the pool leaked through the slab and onto the car parking areas (which are unit subsidiaries), the owners corporation is responsible for ensuring that the leakage is stopped and the area in the carpark below is repaired so that no damage can occur to vehicles parked in the parking areas (unit subsidiaries).

The owners corporation is responsible for all facilities that are used in providing utility services such as plumbing, water, sewerage and electricity (those that benefit all units). In other words, if a plumbing line is damaged in the branch line (not the main line that services all units) and that branch line only services one unit, then the unit owner is responsible regardless of the location of that branch line (i.e. even if it goes outside the boundary of the unit and into common property where it joins the main line).

Further, an owners corporation, by unopposed resolution, can exempt itself from responsibility for some of the examples above, if it does not adversely affect the units. In an A-class development, responsibility for repair and maintenance inside the unit is strictly the responsibility of the unit owner (this includes painting).

With respect to leaks, if you have a leak from a unit on, say, level three into a unit on level two, then in most cases responsibility for repair and maintenance of that leak rests with the unit owner on level three. The only time this would not be the case is if there is a leak in a common pipe that services all units and that leak is finding its way into a unit on the level below. Then that responsibility rests with the owners corporation.

Unit owners are responsible for repairing and maintaining their units. In an A-class development this means everything inside the unit from midway floor, walls and ceilings.

B-class units

B-class units are defined as a piece of land upon which a townhouse has been erected. B-class units are unlimited in height, except for any encroachment above or below ground level by another part of the parcel (unit or development).

In B-class developments, the common property can be as small as one square metre, and is generally the pathways through the general garden areas, main roadway, garbage area, pools, tennis courts or gardens.

In B-class units the owners corporation may resolve by way of a special resolution that responsibility for repair and maintenance including painting can become the responsibility of the owners corporation. This resolution can be as broad or as restrictive as the owners corporation wishes. This resolution can be rescinded by a further special resolution at some time in the future.

In a B-class development, if sewage discharges into a unit because of a tree causing damage to the branch line (and the tree is located on common property) the owner could argue that the owners corporation is responsible as it is the common property tree that caused the damage.

Unit owners are responsible for repairing and maintaining their units. In a B-class development this means everything on the piece of land.

New South Wales

The definition of common property is everything not included in the lot. In NSW the common property walls are those that correspond to the thick lines on the strata plan; fine lines are boundary lines (no structure) and dotted lines are survey lines used by surveyors to determine boundary points. Viculum/viculi are curved lines and link two parts of a unit divided by a common property wall such as courtyards and balconies.

All floors and ceilings are common property and that includes dividing floors in a two-storey townhouse or apartment. All internal stairways are common property as they are considered a floor or ceiling on an angle, such as in townhouses or apartment blocks. Painting, carpeting and wallpaper on common property walls and floors are defined as contents and are not the owners corporation's responsibility.

Always obtain a copy of the strata plan to ensure you understand what is deemed private and common property in your individual strata scheme.

Specific examples

Internal fixtures and fittings

All internal fixtures and fittings such as walls, basins and baths are not the responsibility of the owners corporation to repair and maintain, only to insure. If there is no defined event then there is no claim on fixtures and fittings. If a shower screen cracks through an accident then it is repaired by the owner and an insurance claim is made under common strata insurance. However, if the shower screen door itself is damaged through wear and tear, then it will be up to the owner to repair or replace it.

Floor coverings

All tiles and coverings glued or fixed to the common property at the date of registration of the strata plan are common property. As an example, in a wet area such as a bathroom tiles located on an external wall are common property and will be the responsibility of the owners corporation. The tiles located on the internal walls will be private property and the owner's responsibility to maintain and replace. Tiles that are located on a common property wall will be the responsibility of the owners corporation. However, the shower hob (the raised sill around the shower floor) will generally be private property.

Manholes

These are for access to roofs and are sometimes located in the ceilings of private units. If the manhole is located in a ceiling that is common property, then the manhole will be common property. Under section 65 of the *Strata Titles Act 1996* the body corporate can have access to the unit for any repairs and maintenance issues to common property. An owner cannot prevent access in the case of an emergency but in all other cases the consent of the occupier is required. If that cannot be obtained, an order of an adjudicator for access must be obtained under section 145 of the Act.

Doors

Front doors of units are a part of common property. Garage (roller and tilt) doors are generally common property. The motor is generally part of the lot if it's located within the unit. Wiring is common property if it's located in a common property wall and will be the responsibility of the owners corporation.

Fences

The replacement or repair of a fence dividing common property and a lot is to be shared equally between the owners corporation and the lot owner. The cost to repair or replace any fences between two lot owners is also to be shared equally. The boundary fences of a scheme are generally considered to be common property and therefore the cost of repair or replacement of the fence would be shared between the owners corporation and the neighbouring property. However, it is critical when dealing with fences that you refer to the strata plan and/or the by-laws of the scheme to see if there is some notation contrary to the Act.

Balconies

Generally balconies are common property from the upper to the lower surfaces including tiling, concrete and the water proofing. These are the owner corporation's responsibility. Railing or barriers located on the boundary of the lot balcony are common property because they constitute a wall which corresponds with the boundary line on the plan. Doors leading onto the balcony will usually form part of the lot if in a strata plan registered before 1 July 1974 and common property in a strata plan registered on or after 1 July 1974. Balcony tiles are generally common property and the owners corporation can select the colour, design and style of the tiles to be installed.

Pipes

All pipes, wires and cables in a common property wall are common property. Any pipes which are not located in the lot are common property irrespective of which lot they service. Once those pipes enter a lot they will still be common property if the walls are common property and if they service more than one lot (or form a part of a reticulation or supply system that services more than one lot).

Air-conditioners

If an air-conditioning system is located on common property then it is the owners corporation's responsibility to maintain if no by-law is registered. However, if the air-conditioner is located on private property but the pipes go through a wall that is common property then that section of the pipe is generally the owners corporation's responsibility.

Northern Territory

Strata subdivisions in the NT are known as unit title developments. The current Act governing unit title developments in the NT is the Unit Titles Act. Under the current Act, common property is defined as all of the land which is part of the unit title development but not within a 'unit'.

As a general rule a 'unit' includes: the inner surface of any boundary walls; the upper surface of the floor that connects with any boundary walls and is within the area of the floor plan; and the under surface of the ceiling that connects with any boundary walls and is within the area of the floor plan.

It does not include the area occupied by a vertical structural support, not being a wall, of a building (such as a pillar or column); pipes, wires, cables or ducts in a building not for the exclusive enjoyment of one unit; or structures enclosing such pipes, wires, cables or ducts. These items are therefore considered common property.

In NT legislation, a 'wall' includes a door, window or any other structure that divides a unit from common property or other units.

Important: If the unit's plan defines the boundaries of the units differently, the plan takes precedence and dictates what falls within a unit and what is common property. For example, the plan may specifically include as part of the unit a particular wall, a roof or any pipes or wiring — in which case the unit owner will own those items and will be responsible for any insurance, maintenance and repairs.

Specific examples

Balconies

The structures of a balcony (excluding the internal surfaces) are usually common property whereas the upper surface of the balcony are the owner's responsibility to maintain and replace. The painting of the external part of the balustrade is the responsibility of the corporation. The water waste pipe located in the balcony is usually the corporation's responsibility to maintain.

Pipes

Water pipes, sewage pipes are usually common property and therefore the corporation's responsibility.

Power and phone lines

The main power and phone lines and main common property power box are the corporation's responsibility. However, power boxes located within individual units are the owners' responsibility.

Patios and backyards

The structural foundation of a patio or backyard is deemed common property but the upper surface of that patio or backyard (such as pavers or grass) is the owner's responsibility to maintain.

Fences

All external boundary fences are the corporation's responsibility; however, where dividing fences are located between units, or units and neighbours, or units and common property, the costs are shared equally. The inside surface of a backyard fence is the unit owner's responsibility.

Queensland

Specific examples in multistorey units

Balconies

The structural aspect of a balcony is always deemed to be common property unless specified as an exclusive-use area in the by-laws. The tiles and the painting of the interior of the balcony may be the responsibility of the unit owner; however, the boundary of the unit will need to be determined first.

Where you have a wall on the balcony leading back into the unit, it is usually considered private property. This applies to both residential and commercial properties.

Awnings

Because awnings provide shelter to other units they are deemed to be common property and therefore a body corporate's responsibility.

Balcony railings

Balcony railings and balustrades are always deemed to be common property and are therefore the responsibility of the body corporate.

Walls and slabs

If there is a wall between two units and there are shared utilities in this space such as water pipes and electrical wires, then they would be deemed to be common property.

If there are utilities in the slab or in the area dividing the bottom unit from the one above, then the utilities would be deemed to be common property.

Windows and doors

These are considered to be common property and therefore the body corporate's responsibility to repair and replace.

Utilities

The infrastructure of the building such as the PBAX (phone) service, security wires and cable TV are installed and owned by the body corporate; however, once the utilities cross over the boundary between the common property and the unit, they become the unit owner's responsibility to repair or replace even though the body corporate still owns them. Up to the crossover point it is the body corporate's responsibility.

Specific examples in single-storey units

Residential

If the roof lines are separated then the roof is usually the owner's responsibility. If the roof line is all one, then it is generally the body corporate's responsibility, but it will also depend on how the by-laws have been written.

Commercial

The external wall of a building is common property and usually all parking areas are common property. Commercial is very similar to residential.

Mixed use

This is similar to commercial and residential use but can also involve volumetric plans of subdivision. Volumetric plans are where units can sit outside the existing body corporate's structure. For example, a restaurant or retail shops may not be a part of the body corporate. An owner needs to seek legal advice, particularly when volumetric plans are involved.

South Australia

In South Australian strata schemes, the exterior to the inside wall is common property so all external walls, floors, balconies and the roof are considered common property. The shell is the responsibility of the strata corporation.

In a strata title, the external paint is usually private property. However, if you repair or replace something that benefits only one owner then legislation states that the owner should be responsible for the cost.

Community title properties have by-laws and they will be descriptive. You often find the by-laws will be different from corporation to corporation. The by-laws will be prescriptive, for example the by-law might protect the outward appearance of the property from being altered by an owner in a manner that is inconsistent with the rest of the outward appearance of the strata corporation. In a community title property, balconies are usually private property. Walls, windows, doors and floors are private property.

South Australia also has 'primary strata' properties. These are corporations that house multiple lots over different levels. The plans for these types of properties define the upper and lower boundaries of the lots of the body corporate in the top right corner. Common property is any part of the building that is not part of a lot.

Specific examples

Roofs

The roof of a unit is generally common property and the strata corporation's responsibility to maintain or replace. This is easy to accept when it is under one roof. Sometimes you might have a configuration where you have six units in a strata corporation and two units share a roof, so you have three blocks of two units. These roofs can also be deemed to be common property and hence the responsibility of the strata corporation. However, it can be good policy for the strata corporation to pass a resolution to the effect that because the roof is benefiting only two owners, those owners should pay for the repair or replacement of the roof.

With a community title plan the roof is considered to be private property and the boundary fence is the responsibility of the strata corporation.

Pipes

The main pipes, such as for water, gas and power supply, are common property and therefore the corporation's responsibility to maintain. However, the branches leading from the main line into the lot are considered to be private property and therefore the responsibility of the lot owner.

Fences

Generally boundary fences belong to the unit owner; however, if the boundary fence is partly common property then the owners would share the cost equally for the relevant section.

With a community title plan the boundary fence is the responsibility of the strata corporation.

Air-conditioners

Air-conditioners can be tricky in South Australia. As an example, if the piping of an air-conditioner from, say, unit five runs at the back of the inside cavity of unit six's wall and the pipe connected to unit five bursts, who is responsible for fixing it? The cavity of the walls and the walls themselves are common property but the pipes are for exclusive use so it would be the owner's issue.

Tasmania

All strata schemes in Tasmania contain areas of common property although they are not always obvious. A common scenario is that the buildings are individually owned and part or all of the outside areas, such as shared gardens are common property. Shared stairwells and hallways may also be common property. However, even in the absence of these obvious shared areas, all the areas above and below the boundaries of a lot are common property, as is service infrastructure. If the boundaries of lots are not stated on the strata plan, the boundaries are taken to be the centre of all floors, walls and ceilings.

To understand what an owner owns and what is common property, lot owners should obtain a copy of the strata plan from the Land Titles Office or electronically from the Land Information System Tasmania (LIST) at <www.the list.tas.gov.au>.

Source: Department of Primary Industries and Water 2008, *Strata Living in Tasmania*, 2nd edition.

Specific examples
Balconies

These can be common property or private, depending on what the strata plan states. For example, if the boundary is the centre of the wall and the balcony hangs over the wall then the balcony will be common property.

Fences

Fences are a grey area and have never been tested in court. However, if a block of units are surrounded by common property and there is a fence surrounding the boundary of the body corporate, with no backyards having been created around the block, then this fence could still be the responsibility of each owner to the width of each unit.

Exclusive use

A unit owner can apply for exclusive use of stairs, land, storeroom, etc., through creating by-laws. A majority of members can pass a by-law that grants exclusive use to a unit owner for five years, they then have to apply to re-register the by-law for another five years. These exclusive rights can be revoked at any time. To revoke the exclusive right it only requires a majority vote from the total number of members within the body corporate. The owner under the exclusive right has total responsibility for, and must maintain, this area. The other option is to have the strata plan amended.

Victoria

Specific examples

Foundations and roof

Many Victorian strata plans state something along the lines of, 'The lower boundary of units 1 to 14 (both inclusive) lies one metre below that part of the site which lies within the vertical or near vertical boundaries of the relevant unit'. The upper boundary of each of these units is usually about 15 metres above its lower boundary. In this case the owner is responsible for their roof and the foundations under the floor. In this example, the common property is all the land in the parcel except the land contained in units one to 14. As a purchaser you should be aware of this.

In other strata plans (for single-storey units) areas above and below the units are deemed to be common property and therefore the owners corporation is responsible for the repair and or replacement of the roof and the foundations of the unit. It also means that the owner could not build a second storey without a unanimous approval from the owners corporation, or build something below the surface such as a wine cellar.

Some plans of subdivision state that 'depth limitations do not apply'. This means that the unit owner owns the immediate air space above their unit (to the Commonwealth of Australia boundary). So, providing they obtain a permit they can build another storey onto the existing building. It also means that they own the land down into the ground and can build, for example, a wine cellar, providing a permit can be obtained. So there is no common property above or below the unit.

A plan of subdivision often states the location of boundaries defined by a building's, 'median' (marked 'M' on the plan) and 'exterior face'. The median means that the two owners would share any repair costs of the wall dividing their two units. The exterior face means that the owner is responsible for all works from the plaster through to the paint work on the exterior of the wall, which would include windows, rising damp, concrete cancer repairs or replacement. The 'interior face' means everything from the exterior paintwork through to the plaster and is the owners corporation's responsibility.

If the strata plan states that all the air between floors to ceiling is private, that means anything above the ceiling is common property and anything below the floor is common property. So, if the foundations or roof deteriorate, it would be the owners corporation's responsibility to repair or replace them.

Front fences

If the street-side front fence of a block of units has a private courtyard behind it and the fence adjoins a footpath without any common property between the footpath and the fence, then the fence belongs to the owner of the unit that sits behind the fence. Councils rarely pay for the repair or replacement of a fence attached to an owners corporation, so this is usually left up to the owner.

If there was common property between the fence and the footpath and there was a private courtyard behind the fence, then the cost of repair or replacement would be shared equally between the owner and the owners corporation. If there is common property behind and in front of the fence then it is the owners corporation's responsibility to repair or replace the fence.

Backyards

A common problem that can occur is that a person purchases a unit under the belief that the backyard belongs to the unit, yet the plan of subdivision clearly shows that it is common property. What happens is that over time people install fences on common property to create private backyards for themselves. The problem is that if a person trips, slips or falls and can prove negligence, it will be the owners corporation that is legally responsible, because the area is common property. Yet the owners corporation quite often has no idea that this is common property, or they choose to do nothing about it. A simple and fairly cheap option is for the owners corporation to agree to lease or licence the area to the unit owner.

Gas hot water boiler

In older buildings there may be one or more common property gas hot water systems supplying the whole block of units. Owners therefore have no control over their hot water supply and the costs involved. Due to their age and construction these buildings are also often unable to have separate water meters and gas meters installed. For investors, this means that the unit owner (not the tenant) must pay for the water and gas charges because the meters are considered common property.

Western Australia

Generally strata plans of properties constructed pre-1985 state that the internal floors, ceilings and walls form part of the units (owner's responsibility). The outside structures, such as the windows doors, gutters, down pipes and roof were common property.

Post-1985 strata plans generally indicate that the boundaries of the lot are the external part of the wall (windows, doors, roofs, etc.) and are the lot owner's responsibility. An exception is in multistorey buildings where all the outside is common property and the inner space of the units is private property (the inside walls, floors and ceilings, etc.).

Specific examples

Columns

Within a commercial building, such as offices, there may be columns running through the building. These columns are often deemed to be common property and the responsibility of the strata company, unless specified as part of a particular unit.

Suspended ceilings

The definition of the unit boundaries is usually the upper surface of the floor to the under surface of the ceiling to the inner surface of the perimeter walls. If an owner or tenant has installed a suspended ceiling after the date of registration, the unit boundary may still run to the underside of the original ceiling or upper floor slab. In such cases the new ceiling and any fixtures installed would ordinarily be part of the unit and therefore the owner's responsibility.

Roofs

If the strata plan states that the boundary of the unit is the external surfaces of the building, then the roof is considered part of the unit for which the owner is responsible.

Balconies

Balconies are usually common property, but it's worth checking for your particular unit — they may show up on the strata plans as being part of the unit. If they are the owner's responsibility it means you will be liable for anyone falling off the balcony, the repair of any concrete cancer (which is common in the older buildings), and the repair and maintenance of the balcony railing. Take careful note of the horizontal and vertical boundaries (as depicted on the floor plan) as these are often unique to the particular scheme.

Residential fences

Repair or replacement of dividing fences between two owners is a shared cost and for them to work out. If the fence borders common property then the fence cost is shared between the lot owner and the strata company. Generally most boundary fences are common property. However, always refer back to your strata plan or survey plan for clarification.

Commercial brick walls and fences

As an example, if you are in a front shop, check to see if the boundary is external surface. If it is and you have a brick wall in front of the shop then the shop is responsible for the wall. So if the wall is the face of the block and has letterboxes in it and business signs on it, legally the owner of the wall can have them removed. The owner is also responsible for any costs associated with the wall.

Dispute resolution process, by region

Australian Capital Territory

Any disputes relating to tenants, owners, managers or a body corporate are currently taken to the Magistrate's Court. However, while the Community Title Act is silent on mediation, this should be considered as the first step and only when that avenue has been exhausted should action be taken before the court.

Note: a new civil and administrative tribunal called ACAT is planned to be operational in the ACT in 2009. This tribunal would then become the first resort failing mediation.

New South Wales

The dispute resolution process in New South Wales is two-fold. If the dispute is the result of an owner breaching a by-law, state strata legislation empowers the owners corporation to issue a notice to comply with the by-law. If the owner still fails to comply, the matter will then progress to the Consumer, Trader and Tenancy Tribunal for a penalty, plus the costs associated with failing to conform with the notice to comply.

In other disputes (primarily between occupants) the arguing parties must attempt mediation as a first step. The Office of Fair Trading has qualified mediators who are skilled in dealing with community and strata schemes disputes. Other approved mediators, such as at a Community Justice Centre, may also be used. If that fails, aggrieved parties can then apply to the strata schemes adjudicator or the Consumer, Trader and Tenancy Tribunal to help reach a legally binding resolution.

See <www.fairtrading.nsw.gov.au> for more information.

Northern Territory

The Northern Territory does not have a specialist dispute resolution body that deals with unit title disputes. Applications to resolve disputes must therefore be made to the Local Court under its small claims jurisdiction. A member may bring an action in cases where any of the following events have occurred:

- the Act or the management corporation's by-laws have been breached
- the management corporation has prejudiced an occupier by a wrongful act or omission
- the management corporation has made an unreasonable or unjust decision
- there is a dispute about the occupation or use of a unit or common property.

The court may do one or more of the following:

- try to settle the matter by mediation and arbitration

- request reports or other information from the parties involved

- order that a party take an action to remedy a breach or default or to resolve the dispute

- order that a party stop doing something

- alter the articles (by-laws) of a corporation

- confirm, vary or reverse a decision of the corporation or the committee

- impose a monetary settlement

- order that a corporation refund money to a member

- impose other incidental or ancillary orders.

Source: Northern Territory Consolidated Acts, Unit Titles Act (Section 106).

Note: a review of legislation taking place at the time of writing will most likely change this process. Visit <www.nt.gov.au/justice> for more information.

Queensland

The *Body Corporate and Community Management Act 1997* outlines the Queensland strata dispute resolution process. The Act requires, in many circumstances, that parties attempt self-resolution before referring the matter on. Self-resolution may include communication between the aggrieved parties, writing to the committee or presenting a motion for consideration at a general meeting.

Failing this, the issue may be referred to the office of the Commissioner of Body Corporate Management. Its role is to initially assess applications (requesting more information if necessary) and then to either dismiss it or send it on to one of the department's dispute resolution services. These include mediation, specialist mediation, specialist conciliation, departmental adjudication or specialist adjudication. Adjudicators have the power to investigate matters through a variety of means including conducting interviews and inspecting records and property. An adjudicator's order can be ratified through the Magistrate's Court or, if a question of law arises, appealed to the District Court.

See <www.justice.qld.gov.au/bccm> for more information.

South Australia

In South Australian strata schemes, the strata corporation can intervene in disputes between neighbours where there has been a breach of the corporation's articles (by-laws). This would usually involve the corporation writing to the unit owner or tenant reminding them of the by-laws and noting that they are breaching them by, for example, playing loud music late at night. If the unit owner or tenant feels they have been treated unfairly they may take their case to the Magistrate's Court.

Mediation through a community mediation services is the recommended first step to resolving an escalated dispute in South Australia. Mediators help the parties put together a 'good faith' agreement that is not legally binding. The sessions are private (unlike court proceedings), relatively cheap and can significantly reduce anxiety among the parties involved.

If the dispute involves a tenant (rather than an owner), an application can be made to the Residential Tenancy Tribunal to terminate the tenancy. This might be when a tenant is using a unit for illegal purposes, causing a nuisance or interfering with the reasonable peace, comfort or privacy of other residents.

See <www.courts.sa.gov.au> for more information.

Tasmania

In Tasmania, the Recorder of Titles is responsible for resolving strata-related disputes. Similarly to other states, before someone can apply to the Recorder to hear the matter, the dispute must have been through the strata scheme's internal resolution process as outlined in its by-laws.

Disputes must be lodged using an official form available from the Land Titles Office and the process costs about $25 (at time of writing). The Recorder has an option to hold a hearing or may investigate the matter in a number of other ways including reviewing written submissions or inspecting relevant books, papers and other documents.

Tasmania's Recorder operates much like a tribunal in other parts of Australia. The types of orders it is able to make are similar and its decisions are legally binding. Failure to comply will result in fines upwards of $5000.

Appeals against an order of the Recorder of Titles are dealt with by the Resource Management and Planning Appeal Tribunal.

See <www.dpiw.tas.gov.au> for more information.

Victoria

In Victoria there is a three-stage dispute resolution process:

1   Internal resolution.

2   Conciliation through Consumer Affairs Victoria.

3   Application to the Victorian Civil and Administrative Tribunal (VCAT) for an order.

Internal complaints must be made in writing to the owners corporation and it, in turn, must respond in writing. If the owners corporation is initiating the action, the relevant unit owner must comply within 28 days to avoid further action. The next step would be to issue a final notice (giving the unit owner another 28 days to comply). Failing that, and assuming any other measures stipulated in the owners corporation's internal resolution process have been tried, the owners corporation may then make an application to VCAT. However, an owner, occupier or manager is not required to use the owners corporation's internal process and may take their case directly to Consumer Affairs which will assess whether the matter can be settled by conciliation. However, Consumer Affairs may direct that the dispute first go through an internal dispute resolution process before being heard by VCAT.

The next step is VCAT, which can impose a wide range of penalties including monetary penalties and ordering parties to take a specific action to rectify the issue. An order from VCAT is enforced by the Magistrate's Court.

Log on to <www.consumer.vic.gov.au > and head to the 'Buying and selling property' section for more information.

Western Australia

The WA State Administrative Tribunal (the SAT) is the destination for strata disputes that have escalated beyond the strata scheme. The SAT is entitled to adjudicate over a broad range of strata issues; however, it may not intervene in cases where title to land has come into question.

If a question of law arises out of the SAT cases, the matter may then be appealed to the Supreme Court.

See <www.sat.justice.wa.gov.au> for more information.

Investigating body corporate records before you buy

Australian Capital Territory

In the ACT, vendors must supply potential buyers with a copy of the annual general meeting's minutes, the executive meeting's minutes and financial statements from the preceding two years on request. For access to additional body corporate records, buyers must apply to the vendor, agent or solicitor and, if granted, pay an inspection fee of around $30 to view the documents at a suitable time in the strata manager's office.

New South Wales

In New South Wales the owner must give written authority for another person to inspect the records. A fee needs to be paid, records need to be located and an inspection carried out. A managing agent will not comment on the records; it is up to the inspector to interpret what's written.

Northern Territory

Buyers in the Northern Territory can contact the management corporation manager or secretary via the real estate agent or vendor and request a Section 37 Statement that outlines the financial status of the unit and any outstanding or upcoming fees, such as a special levy, that have been agreed. Section 7 of the Unit Titles Act allows a unit owner to request the books and records of the corporation. There is nothing to prohibit that owner from passing the documents on to prospective buyers.

Queensland

Since July 2006, under the 'conveyancing protocol', contracts of sale in Queensland must include a disclosure statement on the body corporate. The statement includes details such as the balance of the sinking fund, how much the property is insured for and quarterly levy fees.

South Australia

In South Australia, real estate agents generally apply for a Section 139 Statement (Community Titles Act) and Section 41 Statement (Strata Titles Act) when selling units or strata titles. Prospective investors can apply for copies of these statements as well.

Under the legislation, strata corporations face a fine of up to $500 for refusing to supply a statement that must set out a range of details including any arrears in strata levies. Copies of meeting minutes, existing insurance policies and a statement of accounts must also be supplied. Potential buyers need to send the application for a statement to the strata corporation secretary or to any member of the property's management committee.

Tasmania

In Tasmania, new legislation has made it easier for buyers to find out more details on bodies corporate. Under the *Strata Titles Amendment Bill 2006*, investors no longer need approval from the body corporate to obtain a copy of the certificate that contains information about the corporation.

Victoria

Victorian legislation that came into effect on 31 December 2007 has made it easier for buyers to be informed about the owners corporation they are potentially buying into. It mandates that an Owners Corporation Certificate must be attached to the contract of sale (as part of the Section 32). Owners corporations must allow purchasers, or their representative, to access the owners corporation's register. This register includes the name and address of each owners corporation member, leases or licences, records of accounts, minutes of meetings, long-term agreements and details of insurance cover. Some body corporate managers charge a fee to provide copies of the information. All records created after 1 January 2008 are also available for a fee.

Guidebooks on how to search for owners corporation records are available through the Victorian Law Foundation <www. victorialaw.org.au> and Consumers Affairs Victoria <www. consumer.vic.gov.au>.

Western Australia

Residential strata property buyers in WA must seek approval from the vendor to search the strata company details. Under Section 43 of the Strata Titles Act, a proprietor or mortgagee of a unit can make an application in writing and pay a fee, if applicable, to the strata company for access to documents.

Helpful resources

Peak organisations

ACT Strata Managers Institute

<www.smiact.com.au>

The Strata Managers Institute (ACT) Incorporated is the peak industry body for the management of owners corporations in the Australian Capital Territory. Its membership is made up of strata management firms and employees of strata management firms.

Community Titles Institute of South Australia

<www.ctisa.org.au>

CTISA is the peak industry body for strata and community titles management in South Australia. Membership includes body corporate management firms, managers, support staff, industry partners, students and other key stakeholders in this rapidly growing service sector.

Community Titles Institute Queensland

<www.ctiq.org.au>

CTIQ is the peak industry body for body corporate and community title management in Queensland. Membership includes body corporate managers, support staff, committee members and suppliers of products and services to the industry.

Institute of Strata Title Management

<www.istm.org.au>

ISTM is the peak industry body for the strata industry of NSW. Its membership is made up of strata managers and suppliers of products and services to the strata industry.

National Community Titles Institute

<www.ncti.org.au>

The National Community Titles Institute (NCTI) is the Australian representative professional association for homeowners, community associations, body corporate management practitioners, solicitors, tradespeople, insurers, bankers and other parties involved in the professional, full-time administration of community and strata schemes.

Owners Corporations Victoria (OCV)

<www.ocv.org.au>

OCV (formerly IBCMV) is the peak professional association for the body corporate industry in Victoria. It provides a forum for improved standards and education in the industry.

Strata Titles Institute of Western Australia

<www.stiwa.com.au>

STIWA is the peak industry body for people and organisations working in the strata titles profession and associated industries in Western Australia.

Other national organisations

Ace Body Corporate

<www.acebodycorp.com.au>

Ace Body Corporate Management is an international body corporate management company with offices throughout Australia as well as in Singapore.

Andreones, Lawyers

<www.andreones.com.au>

With offices in Melbourne and Sydney, Andreones specialise in strata and community title law, nationally.

Australian Essential Services Group

<www.aesg.com.au>

Australian Essential Services Group (AESG) is a national auditing and compliance company whose main aim is to make your building safe and compliant with the current state and local government regulation.

CHU

<www.chu.com.au>

CHU specialise in strata and community title insurance and have offices in NSW, Victoria, WA, SA and Queensland.

Lannock Strata Finance

<www.lannock.com.au>

Information on funding options in strata. Lannock is a finance company that lends to bodies corporate but the site contains lots of useful information on all three forms of strata funding, including how to decide which form is best in your situation.

Websites: body corporate information

(See also 'Advice and complaint resolution' in this appendix.)

Domain

<www.domain.com.au>

Site primarily for buying and selling property across Australia but also offers some great tips.

Mystrata

<www.mystrata.com>

Helpful website for people who own, live in, work in, build or manage strata properties. Features loads of information and a discussion forum.

realestate.com.au

<www.realestate.com.au>

Another site primarily focused on buying and selling property, which also offers some comprehensive advice for strata property owners and buyers.

Strataman

<www.strataman.com.au>

Offers tips and advice mainly for NSW strata properties but also has some great general information.

Websites: homebuyers

Aussie Home Loans

<www.aussie.com.au>

Aussie offers a mortgage brokerage service that includes its own home loan packages. The website offers a borrowing guide, mortgage calculator and jargon buster among other features.

Australian Property Monitors

<www.apm.com.au>

Australian Property Monitors is a national supplier of online property price information. Its website features various price guide reports from across the country.

eChoice

<www.echoice.com.au>

A home loan broker offering its own products as well. This site offers visitors various calculator functions for home loans, saving, borrowing, stamp duty and home loan comparisons.

Purchasers Strata Inspections Pty Ltd

<www.strata.com.au>

For a fee, PSI carry out strata inspections (sometimes called strata reports) in many locations across Australia.

Residex

<www.residex.com.au>

Residex provides Australian residential property statistics based on sales back to 1901 and offers predictions for future property growth.

RP Data

<www.rpdata.com>

Member-only website that offers comprehensive Australia-wide property information.

yourmortgage.com.au

<www.yourmortgage.com.au>

This site ranks loans, compares interest rates and helps you locate a mortgage broker in your area. It also offers calculators for working out how much you can borrow, compares variable to fixed loans, and the long-term costs of renting versus buying. The site features a stamp duty calculator, negative gearing calculator and capital gains tax estimator.

Wizard Home Loans

<www.wizard.com.au>

Wizard offers a variety of loans to suit buyers, investors, renovators and the self-employed. Rate and repayment calculators are available on the site.

Real estate institutes

Real Estate Institute of the ACT

<www.reiact.com.au>

Address:

Ground Floor, 16 Thesiger Court
Deakin West ACT 2600

Postal address:
PO Box 22
Deakin West ACT 2600

Phone: (02) 6282 4544
Fax: (02) 6285 1960
Email: <admin@reiact.com.au>

Real Estate Institute of New South Wales

<www.reinsw.com.au>

Address:

30–32 Wentworth Ave
Sydney South NSW 2000

Postal address:
PO Box A624
Sydney South NSW 1235

Phone: (02) 9264 2343
Fax (02) 9267 9190
Email: <info@reinsw.com.au>

Real Estate Institute of Queensland

<www.reiq.com.au>

Address:

Real Estate House
21 Turbo Drive
Coorparoo Qld 4151

Postal address:
PO Box 1555
Coorparoo DC Qld 4151

Phone: (07) 3249 7347
Fax: (07) 3249 6211

Real Estate Institute of South Australia

<www.reisa.com.au>

Address:

REI House
249 Greenhill Road
Dulwich SA 5065

Phone: (08) 8366 4300
Fax: (08) 8366 4380
Email: <reisa@reisa.com.au>

Real Estate Institute of Tasmania

<www.reit.com.au>

Address:

33 Melville St
Hobart Tas. 7000

Phone: (03) 6223 4769
Fax: (03) 6223 7748
Email: <reit@reit.com.au>

Real Estate Institute of Victoria

<www.reiv.com.au>

Address:

335 Camberwell Rd
Camberwell Vic. 3124

Postal address:
PO Box 443
Camberwell Vic. 3124

Phone: (03) 9205 6666
Fax: (03) 9205 6699
Email: <reiv@reiv.com.au>

Real Estate Institute of Northern Territory Inc.

<www.reint.com.au>

Address:

Real Estate House
Unit 3, 6 Lindsay Street
Darwin NT 0800

Phone: (08) 89818905
Fax: (08) 89813683

Real Estate Institute of Western Australia

<www.reiwa.com>

Address:

REIWA House
215 Hay Street
Subiaco WA 6008

Phone: (08) 9380 8222
Fax: (08) 9381 9260
Email: <reiwa.com@reiwa.com.au>

Advice and complaint resolution

New South Wales

Consumer, Trader & Tenancy Tribunal

<www.cttt.nsw.gov.au>

Address:

Level 12, 175 Castlereagh Street
Sydney NSW 2000

Postal address:
GPO Box 4005
Sydney NSW 2001

Phone: 1300 135 399
Fax: 1300 135 247

Queensland

Commissioner for Body Corporate and Community Management

<www.justice.qld.gov.au>

Address:

Level 11, 259 Queen Street
Brisbane Qld 4000

Postal address:
GPO Box 1049
Brisbane Qld 4001

Phone: 1800 060 119
Fax: (07) 3227 8023

South Australia

Residential Tenancy Tribunal (Office of Consumer and Business Affairs Tenancies)

<www.ocba.sa.gov.au/tenancies>

Address:

Level 1, 91–97 Grenfell Street
Adelaide SA 5001

Postal address:
GPO Box 965
Adelaide SA 5001

Phone: (08) 8204 9544
Fax: (08) 8204 9570

Tasmania

Recorder of Titles, Land Titles Office, Department of Primary Industries and Water

<www.dpiw.tas.gov.au>

Address:

Level 1, 134 Macquarie St
Hobart Tas. 7000

Phone: (03) 6233 2618
1300 368 550
Fax: (03) 6223 8089

Victoria

Victorian Civil and Administrative Tribunal (VCAT)

<www.vcat.vic.gov.au>

Address:

55 King Street
Melbourne Vic. 3000

Postal address:
GPO Box 5408
CC Melbourne Vic. 3001

Phone: (03) 9628 9800
1800 133 055
Fax: (03) 9628 9822

Western Australia
State Administrative Tribunal
<www.sat.justice.wa.gov.au>
Address:
Level 4, 12 St Georges Terrace
Perth WA 6000

Postal address:
GPO Box U1991
Perth WA 6845

Phone: (08) 9219 3111
1300 306 017
Fax: (08) 9325 5099

Note: There is currently no strata-specific body for complaint resolution in the ACT. Since complaints are heard by the Magistrate's Court, you will need to consult a lawyer in the first instance about advancing your dispute.

Contributors

Australian Capital Territory

Eric Adriaanse
Independent Body Corporate P/L

Jan Browne
Ian McNamee & Partners Real Estate

Peta Ribbens
Strata Managers Institute (ACT) Inc.

New South Wales

Francesco Andreone
Andreones, Lawyers

Bruce Bentley
JS Mueller & Co. (strata lawyers)

Richard Holloway
Richard Holloway Enterprise Pty Ltd

Paul Morton
Lannock Strata Finance

Marc Steen
Trades Monitor

Northern Territory

Roger Bell
Ace Body Corporate Management (Darwin)

Lyn Bennett
Minter Ellison Lawyers

Queensland

David Bugden
Mystrata Pty Limited

Gary Budgen
Mystrata Pty Limited

James Freestun
Solutions IE

Rieta Mistry
Ace Body Corporate Management (Brisbane)

South Australia

Tyson & Florina D'Sylva
Ace Body Corporate Management

Brett Earle
Strata Data Group

Victoria

Rob Beck
Owners Corporation Victoria

Jonathan B Cohen
LMS Lawyers

Leslie G Clements
Clements & Co (lawyers)

Paul Keating
CHU (Corporate Home Unit Underwriting)

Tim Graham
McKean & Park Lawyers & Consultants

Tim McKenzie
Macquarie Bank

Julie McLean
Ace Body Corporate Management (Mentone)

Paul Morton
Lannock Strata Finance

Kim Rockman
AESG (Australian Essential Services Group)

Jenny Wang
Berrigan Doube Lawyers (Vic.) P/L

Western Australia

Mark Atkinson
Atkinson Legal

Robert Kronberger
Atkinson Legal

Ian Laird
Strata Titles Consultant

STEPHEN RAFF
ENTREPRENEUR, AUTHOR,
SPEAKER AND CONSULTANT

Stephen Raff, co-author of best selling books like 'Top Franchise CEO's Secrets Revealed' is a recognised expert in Body Corporate Management. Stephen is also the CEO and founder of Ace Body Corporate Management, one of Australia's largest and most successful body corporate management companies responsible for management of property and assets in excess of $5 Billion.

Ace Body Corporate Management (Ace)

Ace operates 70 franchises across Australia. This geographical reach differentiates Ace from their competitors, by allowing them to provide a more professional and personal management service to each of their customers. All Ace Franchises are individually owned and operated by experienced and qualified personnel.

When dealing with Ace, you can be assured of a superior level of service, combined with the most current and accurate body corporate information and advice.

If you require an effective body corporate management company for your property, contact Ace for a total body corporate solution.

Need advice? Stephen Raff is an expert in all areas of body corporate management. To ensure that you understand all your body corporate management obligations before the purchase of your next property, contact Stephen direct on 0409 586 941 or stephen.r@acebodycorp.com.au

Ace Body Corporate Management Pty Ltd
Phone: (03) 9585 3055 Fax: (03) 9583 8911
106 Nepean Highway, Mentone, Victoria, 3194

ACE BODY CORPORATE MANAGEMENT

PROFESSIONAL PERSONAL SERVICE

Ace Body Corporate Management (Ace) has been in operation since 1995, and is now one of Australia's leading body corporate management companies. Through their network of 70 Franchises, Ace currently manages property and assets in excess of $5 Billion.

Need an effective body corporate management company?

Let Ace provide you with:

- *Experienced and qualified body corporate managers.*
- *Collection and management of all fees and levies.*
- *Body corporate record keeping and administration.*
- *Prompt response to phone calls and enquiries.*
- *Facilitation of financial reports and annual general meetings.*
- *Co-ordination of all building maintenance & repairs.*
- *24X7 Emergency Services.*
- *Qualified mediators.*

Please contact Ace Body Corporate Management to enquire how we can assist you to manage your body corporate.

Ace Body Corporate Management Pty Ltd
Phone: (03) 9585 3055 Fax: (03) 9583 8911
106 Nepean Highway, Mentone, Victoria. 3194